THE
HOME
FRONT

IN PHOTOGRAPHS

THE HOME FRONT

IN PHOTOGRAPHS

LIFE IN BRITAIN DURING THE SECOND WORLD WAR

EMMA CROCKER

SUTTON PUBLISHING

First published in 2004 by
Sutton Publishing Limited . Phoenix Mill
Thrupp . Stroud . Gloucestershire . GL5 2BU

British Library Cataloguing in Publication Data

A catalogue record for this book is available from the British Library.

ISBN 0-7509-3674-6

Endpapers. Front: Evacuees from Bristol, with luggage labels, suitcases and gas masks, arriving at Kingsbridge in 1941. *(IWM D 2593)*
Back: Men and women at work on the production of Merlin engines in the plating shop of the Rolls-Royce factory in 1943. *(IWM D 12122)*

Typeset in Baskerville Mt 12/15 pt
Typesetting and origination by
Sutton Publishing Limited.
Printed and bound in England by
J.H. Haynes & Co. Ltd, Sparkford.

For
Jeremy, Mum, Dad
and Beck

CONTENTS

PREFACE

This book is based solely on the collection of photographs originally compiled by the Ministry of Information (MoI) during the Second World War, which are now held by the Photograph Archive of the Imperial War Museum, London. This series of photographs is known as the 'D Series', the 'D' being the alphabetical prefix given by the MoI to the series of photographs focusing on the civilian experience of war (as opposed to the Navy ('A' prefix) or the Army in the UK ('H' prefix), or in the Far East ('FE' prefix), for example). As will be seen in Chapter 5, originally the MoI simply collated pictures taken by agency photographers, but as the war progressed they commissioned more and more photographers to take pictures for their own purposes.

I decided to focus solely on these official photographs (of which there are over 25,000), rather than including the agency photographs also held by the Imperial War Museum, as I wanted to examine the way in which they reflect not only the ideals of the Ministry but also many aspects of wartime life itself. In addition, the majority of photographs in this series have not been seen in print since their use in wartime publications, so I aimed to throw a spotlight on this rich resource.

This book is intended to offer a general overview of the main themes of the Second World War, with the photographs, as far as is possible, speaking for themselves. It is by no means a comprehensive history of the Home Front, as numerous excellent books already exist on this subject, but it is a showcase of a small proportion of the Imperial War Museum's collection of Home Front photographs, highlighting the everyday life experienced by the public in Britain during the Second World War.

ACKNOWLEDGEMENTS

I would like to thank all at Sutton Publishing, and my work colleagues Janice Mullin, Ian Carter and Alan Wakefield, for their full support of my project from the outset, and Terry Charman for his proof-reading skills. My thanks also go to the Trustees of the Imperial War Museum for granting me permission to use these photographs.

I would very much like to thank my parents and sister for always being there when I need them, for supporting me through university (twice!) and for making me feel guilty about not working on my book by asking me for a progress report on a weekly basis.

Finally, I would like to say a huge thank you to my husband Jeremy for his love and encouragement, for enduring the numerous drafts of my manuscript, for his advice on some of the photographs and, most of all, for surviving my mood swings during writing!

Author's Note
I would like to remind readers that this is not an Imperial War Museum book. Any opinions or views expressed in the following pages are mine alone and are not necessarily those of the Imperial War Museum.

INTRODUCTION
A PRELUDE TO WAR

By the time Prime Minister Neville Chamberlain arrived at Heston Airport on 30 September 1938, clutching a piece of paper that he proclaimed signalled 'peace for our time', the seeds for the Second World War had been well and truly sown. Since his rise to power in 1933 Adolf Hitler and his National Socialist party had been gradually attempting to increase the territory governed by Germany. The Saar returned to Germany after a plebiscite in March 1935 and the Rhineland was reoccupied the following year; Austria was annexed in the spring of 1938 and the Sudetenland in October 1938. Chamberlain attempted to resolve the situation by meeting with Hitler, Mussolini of Italy and Daladier of France in Munich. It was his third visit to Hitler that September. In an attempt to preserve peace, Chamberlain bowed to Hitler's demands and Czechoslovakia was also annexed to Germany in March 1939.

The paper that Chamberlain carried renounced any warlike intentions against Britain by Germany. However, after having signed an alliance with Poland on 25 August 1939, Britain was obliged to support Poland after her invasion by Germany on 1 September. Britain issued Germany with an ultimatum, which expired at 11 a.m. on 3 September.

The growth of fascism in Germany, Italy and Spain had been steady during the 1930s, giving cause for concern to many across Europe. Air Raid Precautions were commenced in 1933, and from 1938, when a war with Germany seemed unavoidable, gas masks were produced and the evacuation of civilians from vulnerable areas was planned.

Chamberlain's attempts to appease Hitler and stave off the inevitable war had failed, and at 11.15 a.m. on 3 September 1939 the Prime Minister announced that Britain was at war with Germany.

Neville Chamberlain arrives at Heston Airport on 30 September 1938, brandishing a piece of paper which, he proclaimed, offered a real chance for peace. But Chamberlain's attempts to appease Hitler were unsuccessful, with Czechoslovakia falling into German hands, and less than a year later Britain and Germany were at war. *(IWM D 2239)*

CHAPTER 1

INDUSTRIAL
EVOLUTION
INDUSTRY DURING THE
SECOND WORLD WAR

Perhaps more than any other aspect of the Home Front, industry was essential to the success of the war effort, providing the backbone for campaigns on various fronts. The phrases 'total war' and 'people's war' are frequently used to describe the Second World War, and industry is one of the major factors illustrating these concepts. Men and women from all areas of the Commonwealth were drafted in to participate in the war effort through industry, and British women, more than ever before, were being employed in huge numbers to work in factories of all types.

Britain had always been a seafaring nation, leading the world markets in the late nineteenth and early twentieth centuries. However, the depression during the interwar period, with mass unemployment in many industries (including shipbuilding), meant that the state of the industry in 1939 was in no way conducive to the creation of a successful war machine. Nevertheless, the war brought employment to this depressed industry, and new technologies were developed to cope with demand. Production of ships began to depart from the traditional craft approach, with many parts being prefabricated. One of the most prevalent jobs in shipyards during the Second World War was that of the riveter, who received the highest wages of all shipyard employees. This caused problems in the yards, as many of the riveters were women. The number of women

Opposite:
A ship skeleton at a British shipyard in 1944. Ships were extremely important to the war effort, not only as the Royal Navy's contribution to the British war machine but also as a means to transport troops, food and equipment.
(IWM D 20825)

A riveter at work in a British shipyard, c. 1944. Shipbuilding was revolutionised during the Second World War, with the use of prefabricated steel panels joined together with rivets becoming much more widespread. Shipbuilding was one of the many reserved occupations, which meant that employees were exempt from conscription.
(IWM D 18324)

employed in shipbuilding rose drastically from 3,000 in 1938 to 24,000 in 1944. Overall, prefabrication sped up the production of vessels, and also made repair much easier. The importance of British shipyards can be seen in their output: between 1939 and June 1944 more than 700 major warships, 5,000 small craft and 4.5 million tons of merchant shipping had been produced.

Aircraft were, of course, essential to the success of the war effort, a fact particularly apparent during the Battle of Britain in 1940. The Ministry of Aircraft Production (MAP) was led by Lord Beaverbrook between May 1940 and June 1941, and under his leadership aircraft production rose at an astonishing rate from 3,000 in 1938 to 15,000 in 1940, finally reaching 26,461 in 1944. Before the war aircraft production had been carried out on a much smaller scale: in 1935 the total number of people working in the industry was 35,000, but by 1944 each individual aircraft factory employed between 3,000 and 15,000 people. In all, around 120,000 aircraft were built during the war years. Most wartime aircraft production continued to use a group of firms which included A.V. Roe, Vickers and Rolls-Royce, but many people also worked as piece- or out-workers to produce several of the various parts needed in aircraft construction.

A propeller being fitted to a Bristol Beaufighter Mark X under construction, probably at Bristol's shadow factory at Old Mixon, Weston-super-Mare, 1944. Of the 5,500 Beaufighters that entered service during the Second World War, 3,116 were built at Old Mixon. Beaufighters were used by RAF Coastal Command as anti-shipping strike aircraft and were torpedo-equipped. *(IWM D 21107)*

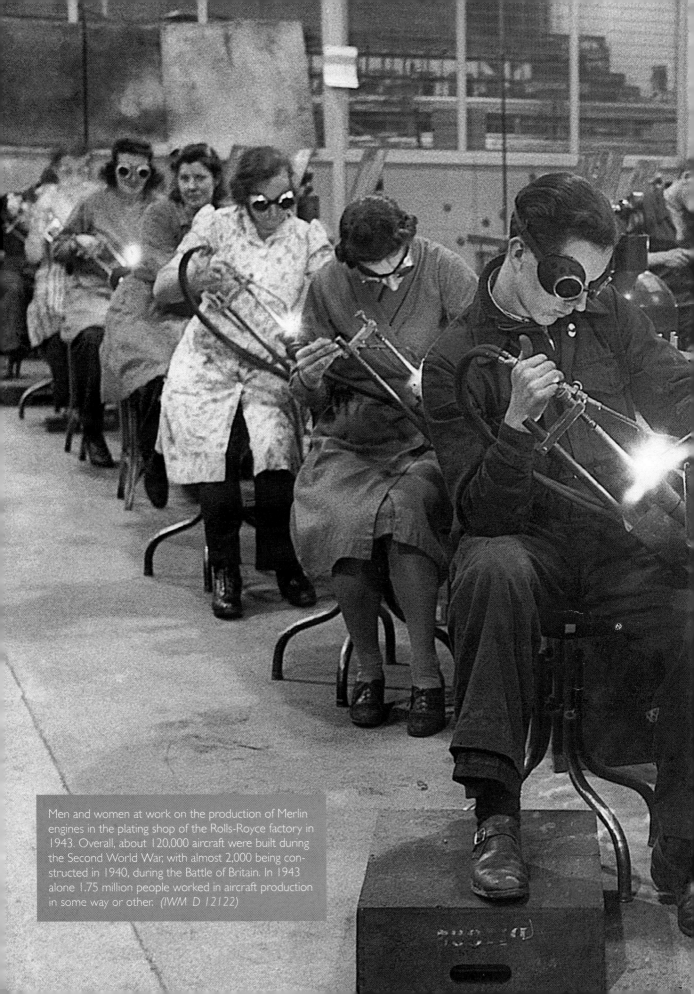

Men and women at work on the production of Merlin engines in the plating shop of the Rolls-Royce factory in 1943. Overall, about 120,000 aircraft were built during the Second World War, with almost 2,000 being constructed in 1940, during the Battle of Britain. In 1943 alone 1.75 million people worked in aircraft production in some way or other. *(IWM D 12122)*

A Matilda tank nears completion at a factory somewhere in Britain, probably in July 1942. The tank tracks remain to be fitted. According to the original MoI caption, one tank took about 2,000 man-hours to build. The year 1942 saw tank production soar, with the week beginning 22 September being designated 'Tanks for Russia' week: all tanks produced that week were destined for the Russian Front. (IWM D 9191)

Once the Battle of Britain was won, attention could be turned to tank production. Although put on the back-burner until 1941, tank production continued in earnest under the direction of Lord Beaverbrook, who had moved from the MAP in June 1941 to become Minister of Supply (being replaced at the MAP by Sir Stafford Cripps in November 1942). Many tanks were produced for the Russian Front in 1942. Indeed, all the tanks produced between 22 and 29 September 1942 were destined for Russia, and in total 8,600 were built in this year. However, despite extensive efforts, many tanks were faulty and Britain relied heavily on American Lend-Lease tanks.

In addition to the heavy hardware of war (ships, aircraft and tanks), the smaller but no less important items such as bullets, shells, rifles and torpedoes were also produced in their millions. Indeed, the number of people working in munitions production had increased from 1.25 million in 1939 to 8.5 million in 1943. Buildings of all sizes and purposes, including showrooms, living rooms and garden sheds, were converted for use as munitions factories, or for the production of other vital equipment such as communication cables, fuses and other aircraft, tank or vehicle parts.

Coal was essential for all war industry and also for domestic fuel. Mining, like shipbuilding, had always been a 'family business', with many generations following their forebears into the pits. Unfortunately, again like shipbuilding, it was a depressed industry, high in absenteeism and strikes, and one whose ageing workforce was causing output to decrease. Younger workers were brought in to replace them, but they quickly became frustrated and moved on to other jobs, thus causing numbers to diminish and output to decline even further. In 1939 there were 766,000 miners, but by 1941 this figure had decreased to fewer than 700,000, despite an Essential Works Order being placed on the coal industry. All men with previous mining experience were registered and recalled to the industry. The figure rose slightly to 709,000 in 1942, and then remained static until the end of the war.

Mrs Coleman, Miss Brearley and a colleague fit woollen jackets to the glass flasks of 'sticky bombs'. Coated with adhesive and filled with explosives, when thrown the adhesive enabled the bomb to stick to the target before detonation. The production of bombs, bullets and torpedoes was just as important as the hardware of war: without ammunition, ships, tanks and guns would be useless in the field. (IWM D 14761)

This view of the assembly floor of a tank factory shows the sheer scale of production: in 1942 alone over 8,500 tanks were produced. British tanks were never quite as successful as American-made models, with many proving unreliable in the sandy conditions of the Western Desert. *(IWM D 4501)*

PLEASE KEEP CLEAR

Miners leave the pit at the end of their shift at
a 200-year-old colliery in the Midlands. Over 700,000
men worked in the coal industry during the Second
World War, providing essential fuel for domestic and
industrial use. Coal was fundamental to the success of
the war effort on every level, as it was also used to fuel
warships. The inability of the industry to keep up with
demand meant that fuel economy was exceedingly
important. *(IWM D 18877)*

In an attempt to keep up the numbers of miners Minister of Labour Ernest Bevin developed the 'Bevin Boy' scheme in 1943. This meant that conscripted men were balloted so that a certain number were directed into mining rather than into the forces (with the exception of those accepted as submarine crew or aircrew, and those in highly skilled occupations). The scheme resulted in 21,000 balloted men working in the mines. In addition, many others volunteered to work in the coal industry, boosting numbers still further. Even so, supply could not keep up with demand, and in 1942 there was an attempt to ration coal. Fuel economy was therefore an essential part of the war effort, and was vigorously encouraged through various MoI exhibitions and campaigns.

The largest change in all industries (and also, as will be shown later, in agriculture and in the armed forces) was the increased involvement of women. Before the war women made up one-third of the 21 million working population. During the war another 2 million women found employment in industry, and various schemes were developed to encourage further participation, such as the provision of childcare and British Restaurants. By 1944 over 7 million of the 16 million women between 14 and 59 years of age were employed in industry, Civil Defence or in the Services.

As we have seen, many men and women worked day and night, both in huge factories and also in their living rooms, garages and sheds, each contributing their own essential part towards the success of the British war effort.

The welfare of war workers, with regard both to their health and to their morale, was extremely important in the propagation of the war effort: a happy and healthy worker was, it was hoped, a good and hard worker! Here three workers at a Royal Ordnance Factory consult the social activities noticeboard in the hostel attached to the factory. Many factories had extensive welfare facilities, including clinics and libraries. *(IWM D 6234)*

George Butler and a colleague set up an Archdale Vertical Miller at an underground factory, somewhere in the English countryside. The factory was situated in a disused quarry and covered an area of almost a million square feet. It offered workers a library, a community hall and other welfare facilities. *(IWM D 9361)*

War work was not restricted to British nationals. Men and women from all over the Commonwealth were drafted in to assist in the war effort, both in providing supplies and goods in their own countries and also as workers in Britain. India sent a huge number of workers to Britain, including this man working in manufacturing. *(IWM D 5923)*

Opposite: Many buildings were adapted to cater for war workers, including garden sheds and even redundant henhouses. Here we see a furniture showroom in Surrey providing space on an upper floor for the winding of armature coils. Many of these part-time workers were trained on site, while the business of selling furniture continued below. *(IWM D 12591A)*

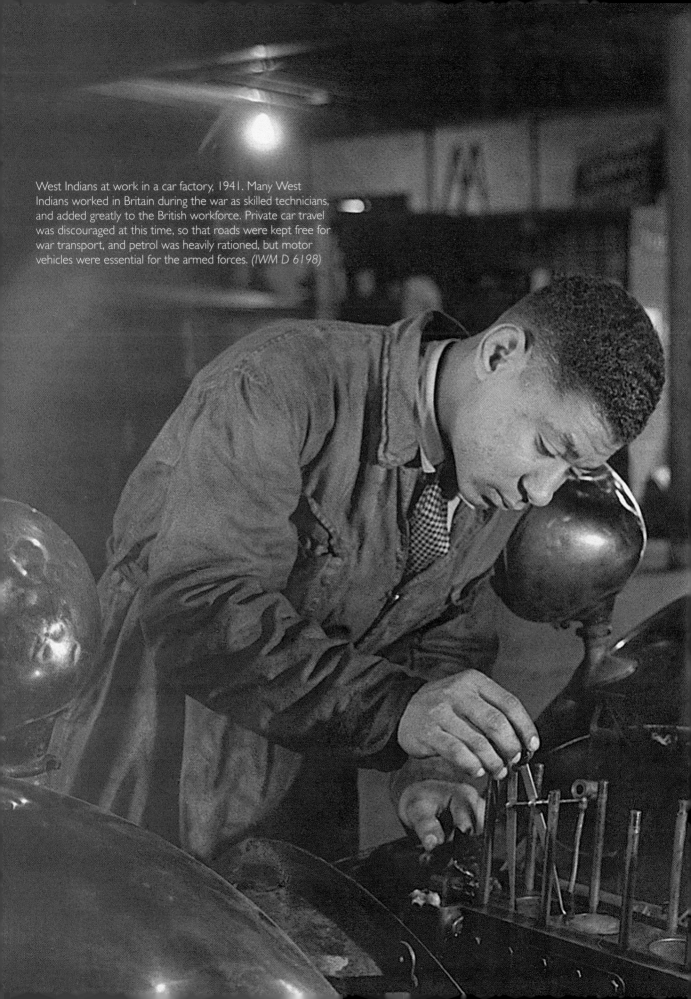

West Indians at work in a car factory, 1941. Many West Indians worked in Britain during the war as skilled technicians, and added greatly to the British workforce. Private car travel was discouraged at this time, so that roads were kept free for war transport, and petrol was heavily rationed, but motor vehicles were essential for the armed forces. *(IWM D 6198)*

War work did not just take place in traditional factories. These part-time female workers are preparing communication cables in the Inspection Room of a factory converted from a peacetime country house, the fireplace providing us with an indication of the room's previous incarnation. The house belonged to Mr and Mrs Clark and every part of the house and garage was given over to the production of telephone apparatus. *(IWM D 12160)*

One of the major impacts on British society was the increased importance of the role of women in trade and industry. Here female carpenters are working at a workshop in 1941. Other photographs in this sequence show windows being constructed, particularly important in replacing those destroyed during air raids. (IWM D 2689)

Milking in progress at Parsonage Farm, 1942. According to the original MoI caption, an average of 190 gallons of milk were produced a day at Parsonage Farm. The cows here were rationed according to their milk production, in order to make the best use of scarce animal feed. *(IWM D 10227)*

CHAPTER 2

ON ENGLAND'S GREEN AND PLEASANT LAND
AGRICULTURE DURING THE SECOND WORLD WAR

Britain had long been an agricultural society and many Second World War writers and information posters celebrated the rural landscape, with several suggesting that it was one of the most important things that soldiers, sailors and airmen were fighting to preserve. At the beginning of the war there were about 17 million acres of grassland and 12 million acres of arable land, and the vast majority of work was done by hand or by horse: only 56,000 tractors were in use in Britain in 1939. With the outbreak of war, and the end of imports from various countries, British farmers faced the difficult task of providing food for both the military and civilian populations. At this time the farming industry was in severe depression, and even in 1943 many farms still did not have the benefit of water and electricity supplies. In addition, many young farmers had enlisted almost immediately at the outbreak of war, and this, coupled with the low wages available in agricultural work, had reduced the labour force.

This led to the revival in June 1939 of the Women's Land Army, which had been active during the First World War. Seen today as the epitome of wartime agriculture, the WLA operated on a voluntary basis, expanding from about 1,000 volunteers at the start of the war

A member of the Women's Land Army is trained in the traditional horse-drawn method of ploughing at the WLA training centre at Cannington, Somerset, c. 1940. All members of the WLA spent time at Cannington or other similar training centres before being posted to farms across the country. (IWM D 118)

Members of the Women's Land Army make hay at Hollow Moor Farm in Mount Batten, Devon, 1942. The WLA built on its First World War roots and at its peak employed over 80,000 women. This kind of view is seen as the epitome of British agriculture in the 1940s: the WLA enjoying long hot sunny days on England's green and pleasant land. *(IWM D 10307)*

to 20,000 in the late summer of 1941, and reaching 80,000 or so in 1944. Tasks carried out by the women of the WLA were extremely varied, as was the welcome they received at the farms and horticultural establishments to which they were assigned. Although one usually associates the WLA with arable farming, and particularly with the harvesting of wheat and other crops, a quarter of WLA activity actually focused on dairy farming, and milking in particular.

The Timber Corps was formed in 1942, and provided about 6,000 members of the WLA with work in sawmills and in felling trees. Such tasks were also carried out by members of the British Honduran Forestry Unit. Many other Commonwealth groups travelled to Britain to help in the war effort, and were particularly useful in agricultural tasks, as well as in industry (see Chapter 1).

Another aspect of WLA work that is frequently forgotten is its role as rat-catcher. With a rat population of 50 million in 1940, which could eat its way through 2.5 million tons of food in a year, rat-catching was an essential part of agricultural life. Over 1,000 members were engaged on this task, and a sequence of photographs in the 'D Series' demonstrates perfectly the many forms this role took, including searching out rat nests, putting down bait and setting traps.

Men of the British Honduran Forestry Unit cut timber somewhere in Britain in 1941. Many workers were drafted in from British Honduras (now Belize) to work in forests in Scotland. Timber was extremely important, and many WLA members were employed in the Timber Corps to produce pit props from logs.
(IWM D 6382)

In addition to these tasks, some WLA members were involved in land drainage and reclamation, land clearance and thatching, with many quickly learning the traditional skills of craftsmen.

Probably the most important part of the agricultural year is harvest time. This was a demanding job. Every available individual pitched in to help, and the WLA, members of the local community, British soldiers and GIs all did their bit to bring in the harvest. Many prisoners of war held in Britain at this time were employed in agriculture, and were particularly important at harvest time. A large number of the photographs in the 'D Series' focus on the harvesting of wheat, as it was such an important crop. The more wheat that could be produced at home, the less that had to be imported. This was very important because it was necessary to limit the amount of foodstuffs being transported (see Chapter 7).

Women were not just assigned to farms. Many WLA members worked in various horticultural research establishments, such as Kew

One of the less well-publicised tasks carried out by members of the WLA was rat-catching. With a rat population of 50 million in 1940 these women clearly had their work cut out! Here we see two Land Girls preparing rat poison, under the supervision of the farmer responsible for training them. The farmer is holding a gun which was used to smoke rats out of their nests.
(IWM D 11221)

In order to make as much land as possible available for arable farming, huge areas had to be drained. Here Land Girls accompany other workmen in excavating and levelling land along a riverbank, c. 1942. *(IWM D 9782)*

At harvest time it was all hands to the pump, and here are some British soldiers lending a hand on a farm somewhere in England, c. 1941. There were Harvest Camps where town children would stay in order to help with the harvest, and it wasn't only farmland that was used to grow wheat: huge swathes of the Sussex Downs and many large parks were also used, providing extra space for this much-needed crop. *(IWM D 4905)*

Opposite: Harry King, aged 71, from Manuden in Essex, prepares to thatch a hayrick. According to the original MoI caption, entitled 'Old Age Pensioner's War Effort', over 700,000 pensioners were engaged in some form of war work. The caption also stated that Mr King had served as a sergeant during the Boer War, and he worked 'a full farming day'. *(IWM D 9246)*

Above: Prisoners of war of all nationalities helped the British war effort (in a roundabout way) by working in agriculture. Here we see a group of German PoWs conferring with the farmer who is employing them, before embarking on a programme of ploughing. By the end of the war more than 90,000 German and 130,000 Italian PoWs were working on the land. *(IWM D 26728)*

A great number of agricultural developments were made during the Second World War, and not just in the fields. At Kew Gardens in London research was carried out into new agricultural technologies. Here chips of potato are sown. Research showed that the yield from these slices was better than that from seed potatoes. It also saved potatoes, as more could be grown from less. *(IWM D 16490)*

Gardens, helping, for example, to develop hardier potatoes, or types that could be grown from chips of potato rather than from seed.

The war did much to modernise British agriculture, leading to a widespread mechanisation that would probably not have happened at the rate it did had the country not been on a war footing. As an example of this, the number of tractors rose dramatically from 56,000 at the start of the war to 203,000 in January 1946. Although horses still outnumbered tractors at this point, the face of British agriculture had begun to change. Indeed, the face of the landscape had also changed, as the proportion of grazing to arable land highlighted at the beginning of this chapter had been drastically altered: by 1944 there were 11 million acres of grassland and 18 million acres of arable. In addition, British farmers were successful in their contribution to the war effort, and (according to an original MoI photograph caption) provided Britons with food for six days of the week.

However, agriculture was not just the preserve of farmers. Civilian allotments were an essential part of food production during the Second World War, providing an important supplement to the

Although horses were still used a great deal in agriculture, the need for more crops led to a great deal of mechanisation. Here, Farmer Hill oversees three of his four tractor ploughs at work on his farm in Kingston Blount, Oxfordshire, 1941. (IWM D 5056)

civilian ration. The 'Dig for Victory' campaign was extremely important during the war, and people of all ages were encouraged to grow their own fruit and vegetables. The number of allotments in England and Wales rose from just over 800,000 in 1939 to nearly 1.5 million in 1945. Many people also kept pigs and rabbits for food, and chickens for their highly prized eggs (see Chapter 9). This widespread use of back yards, window boxes and Anderson shelter roofs to grow food illustrates the fact that agriculture was no longer the sole preserve of the farming community, and represents yet another symbol of the 'people's war' nature of the Second World War.

Attacks on merchant convoys and the need to transport troops, arms and equipment limited the importation of various foodstuffs, so sugar beet was grown extensively in order to replace the usually imported cane sugar. The sugar beet was processed in large factories, being dried out and granulated so that it could be used in the same way as cane sugar. *(IWM D 10898)*

Even London's largest and most famous stores fell victim to air raids. Here we see the remains of John Lewis on Oxford Street in 1940. This gutted building had to be demolished, and the site was later used to host the huge 'Army' exhibition, produced by the MoI, that travelled around the country (see also p. 80). (IWM D 1093)

CHAPTER 3

THE BLITZ

The Zeppelin raids of the First World War had served as a portent of the shape of warfare to come, and the air raids experienced by Britain during the Second World War, although they never achieved the total devastation predicted and feared in the 1920s and 1930s, truly brought the war home to the population on a massive, yet personal, scale. Everyone, civilians and politicians alike, believed that an intensive and overwhelming attack from the air would occur as soon as war broke out. Indeed, pre-war planning had envisaged the resulting casualties numbering 1.75 million dead and over 3.5 million injured, and local authorities ordered in supplies of cardboard coffins to deal with the large numbers of potential corpses. This, however, did not happen, and the period known as the 'Phoney War' (so-named because nothing really happened on the Home Front) began instead. This period of inactivity dragged on until the first air raids of the war hit the north of England and London in the late summer of 1940. The first major raids on London took place on 7 September 1940, predominantly focusing on the East End and docklands area. The bombing continued for another 76 nights and caused nearly 10,000 deaths.

Many of Britain's other cities also suffered air raids. Coventry was perhaps the most famous of them, and the most badly affected in one raid. It was attacked on 14 November 1940, and the devastation caused in this 11-hour raid led the Germans to coin the terms 'Coventration' and 'Coventrated' to signify the complete and utter destruction of a city. In all, 554 people were killed and 1,000 houses destroyed in a raid which was largely unexpected and which re-ignited the pre-war fear of annihilation from the skies. However, within six weeks war production in the city had returned to normal.

Plymouth, Manchester, Merseyside, Clydeside, Birmingham and Hull were among the other cities that faced devastating air raids, but it

This hollow shell, seen from the west tower, is all that remained of Coventry Cathedral after its devastation by German bombs on 14 November 1940. A cross of charred roof beams erected where the high altar once stood is just visible. This photograph was taken in the spring of 1944, after the bulk of the debris had been cleared. *(IWM D 18096)*

wasn't just large industrial cities that were targeted by the *Luftwaffe*. The 'Baedeker Raids' of 1942 focused on those cities featured in the Baedeker tourist guidebooks, and York, Canterbury, Exeter, Norwich and Bath all found themselves in the shadow of the bombers.

In addition to the bombers, the inhabitants of London and the Home Counties also had to face the pilotless V1 flying bombs ('Doodlebugs') and V2 rockets. The V-weapons (the V stands for *Vergeltung*: the German word for 'retribution') began their assault in 1944, with the first V1 landing on Britain in June and the first V2 in September. Croydon fared particularly badly in these attacks, with a total of 142 V1s landing there. By the time the last V-weapons fell on Britain in March 1945, they had between them killed over 7,000 people and injured 22,000.

The provision of some form of air raid shelter was, of course, paramount, and although surface shelters had been erected at the beginning of the war many citizens felt that these were unsafe and preferred to stay in their own homes. Indeed, many of the surface shelters *were* unsafe, as poor-quality mortar meant that many would not withstand the shockwaves from a distant air raid, let alone a direct hit.

Rescue workers search through the rubble after a devastating V1 attack at Upper Norwood in London. The V1 flying bomb (or 'Doodlebug') first hit Britain in June 1944 and its reign of terror continued until March 1945. In total, over 6,700 V1s were seen over Britain during the Second World War. *(IWM D 21211)*

PC Frederick Godwin, stationed at Gipsy Hill in London, supplies tea and sympathy to a now homeless man after a V1 attack that sadly killed his wife and destroyed his house. He returned from taking his dog for a walk to find a scene of devastation. Almost the entire street in Upper Norwood had been destroyed. *(IWM D 21215)*

This photograph of an Anderson shelter in Birmingham in 1940 shows how successful these shelters actually were in doing their job. Although damaged in an air raid, as the nicks in the corrugated steel show, the shelter is still intact and would have protected any inhabitants sufficiently to prevent injury. *(IWM D 4141)*

This Morrison shelter is still intact after a test to prove its strength, *c.* 1941. Morrison shelters enabled citizens without gardens to feel safe during air raids, providing an indoor refuge from falling masonry. They also doubled as very sturdy tables when not in use as shelters! *(IWM D 2300(4))*

Ministers had preferred the evacuation option, encouraging people to leave danger areas completely, as they wished to avoid any form of shelter mentality, whereby the population would retire to bunkers and not emerge until the end of the war. The development of the Anderson shelter was intended to avoid this. People could stay in their own homes and continue life as normal, knowing that there was a safe shelter nearby that they would retreat to in the event of an air raid. Indeed, many evacuees returned to the danger areas during the 'Phoney War', so shelters near home were of the utmost importance. The Anderson shelter was a cheap and easily produced corrugated steel construction, and was named after Dr David Anderson, the engineer who designed it (and not, as is widely believed, after Sir John Anderson, the Home Secretary of the time). These shelters could accommodate several adults and would survive almost anything but a direct hit. They were provided flat-packed, and householders had to dig a large hole in their garden and construct the shelters themselves. Over 2.25 million Anderson shelters were provided free of charge to those with annual incomes of less than £250. Although they were highly successful in protecting their occupants (and in providing a good place for a vegetable patch!), they were not the most comfortable, or popular, of shelters, having a tendency to flood, and they were only suitable for people with gardens.

The Morrison shelter, named after Herbert Morrison, the Minister of Home Security (and later Home Secretary), provided a more 'socially inclusive' alternative (in that no garden was necessary). Used as tables during the day, these shelters offered householders an indoor refuge under a large steel plate. Once again they were handed out free of charge, this time to families with an annual income of less than £350, and by November 1941 over 500,000 had been made available.

Large public shelters were provided in towns and cities to offer protection to those 'caught in the open', either as surface shelters or in the basements of shops and so on, although the government wished to avoid any large concentrations of people, if they possibly could, and continued to advocate the idea of evacuation and dispersal. Despite the improvements made to surface shelters, the vast majority of people preferred the idea of deep shelters, as they felt a lot safer underground, largely because the noise of the bombs falling was muffled. This led to probably the most famous of wartime phenomena, the use of the London Underground as a mass air raid shelter. Although the Tube had offered some shelter during the Zeppelin raids of the First World War, it only began to be used

Perhaps the most famous of all air raid shelters, the London Underground. At its peak in September 1940 it offered safety to 177,000 people. This photograph shows the conditions at Aldwych tube station, with shelterers lining both the platform and the tracks. (IWM D 1675)

Right: The WVS provided tremendous support to those affected by air raids and those tasked with helping them. Here a WVS mobile canteen provides refreshments to members of the Pioneer Corps. Many WVS canteens were donated by other countries, such as the West Indies and Kenya. *(IWM D 2165)*

Below: Welfare Centres were set up across the country to help those made homeless by air raids. Although posed by MoI models, this photograph illustrates the facilities offered in such centres: food, shelter and some-where to wash and sleep. Welfare officers were also on hand to advise newly homeless citizens on their options. *(IWM D 10405)*

for large-scale sheltering in September 1940. The belief that the Tube shelterers developed into some form of community appears to be borne out by the photographs, and indeed 'community' newspapers were in existence. Many Tube stations also had some form of health centre, developed from the original first aid posts provided by the local authorities. However, it is wrong to suggest that everyone who used the Tubes for shelter enjoyed the experience, and equally wrong to say that it was a widespread thing, with every Londoner flocking to his or her local Tube station every night. Although 177,000 civilians did seek shelter in the London Underground, this figure represents only 4 per cent of those in need of shelter at this time. Indeed, communal shelters of all kinds were used by only 9 per cent of the population.

Other subterranean areas were also used as shelters, the most famous of these being Chislehurst Caves in Kent, which are now open to the public. These caves provided even more of a community than the London Underground, boasting two churches, a Citizen's Advice Bureau and a hospital among its facilities.

The devastation and disruption caused by the air raids needed to be cleared up as quickly as possible in order to return the cities to some semblance of normality. Various Civil Defence organisations contributed to the clear-up operations, as did the several power

A father and son play chess to pass the time in this basement shelter in London, while other shelterers read, play cards or try to sleep. This photograph is part of a sequence taken by prominent photographer Bill Brandt in 1940, when he travelled to various shelters across London to record the phenomenon for the MoI. *(IWM D 1520)*

Communal feeding was hugely important after an air raid, as many homes would have no running water, no gas and no electricity. Food (and the people to prepare it) was therefore needed on a large scale. This recipe for bacon roly-poly states that it serves fifty, and it requires 3lb of bacon! This photograph was taken at a training school for those beginning work in communal feeding centres.
(IWM D 22518)

companies, working to restore gas, electricity and water supplies to citizens. The WVS (Women's Voluntary Service) was a key player in the success of rescue and clear-up programmes, providing refreshments to those who had been bombed-out and to Civil Defence workers and fire service members. Canteens and ambulances were donated to the WVS by various overseas organisations and individuals, as their contribution to the war effort. Welfare Centres were opened up to give bombed-out people a temporary roof over their heads and advice on what to do next. Repair squads moved in and worked long and hard to fix roofs and install windows, and temporary camps were even set up for the vast numbers of builders who travelled from all areas of the country to work.

One can only begin to imagine what life must have been like for people at this time. Today, despite the threat of international terrorism, we are, on the whole, safe from such widespread devastation and the constant fear of raids. How well could today's generation cope in similar circumstances?

In order that business could continue in areas that had been badly affected by air raids, emergency telephone bureaux were set up to provide a base where telephone calls could be made and messages received. Messengers were employed to take telephone messages to the offices of which telephone lines had been destroyed. *(IWM D 6420)*

The utilities were often badly affected by the bombing and it was the job of repair squads to reconnect them as soon as possible in order that everyday life could continue as usual. Here we see the gas supply being reconnected as life goes on around the workers in London in 1940. (IWM D 1467)

Tarpaulins are laid to protect the interior of a bomb-damaged house against the elements. The air raid that affected this house clearly also damaged the rest of the houses in the street. This photograph is part of a sequence following 3,000 builders who travelled to London from the north and east of England to help repair bomb-damaged buildings in 1944. These builders were billeted in specially constructed hostels in Onslow Square in the centre of London's Belgravia. By January 1945 some 130,000 repairmen were at work in London. *(IWM D 21295)*

CHAPTER 4

THE PROTECTORS

THE WORK OF

CIVIL DEFENCE

ORGANISATIONS

People living in Britain during the Second World War lived with the threat of air raids and in constant fear of invasion, and thus it was important that the UK had an efficient civil defence system in place. Civil Defence as an organisation came into being in September 1941 and was made up of Air Raid Precautions (ARP) and the National Fire Service. In addition, the Home Guard was another important aspect of civil defence.

Plans for some form of Air Raid Precautions had been on the drawing board since the 1920s, following the Zeppelin raids on London during the First World War. One of the major aspects of ARP training involved dealing with gas attacks. An anti-gas school was opened at Falfield in Gloucestershire in April 1936, and at the end of that year, amid accusations of 'scaremongering', a gas mask factory was established in Lancashire. In 1937 the Air Raid Precautions Act was passed obliging all local authorities to cooperate with government ARP plans. In return, the government would issue grants of between 60 and 75 per cent of the costs of Civil Defence in each area, which included anti-gas equipment and clothing. In 1938 some 38 million gas masks were issued, and gas masks for babies were also developed, although they were not available initially.

Air Raid Precautions included air raid wardens, first aid posts, rescue squads and fire-watchers. The ambulance service and fire services also

Although they were not issued immediately during the Munich Crisis of September 1938, gas masks for babies were developed and were in widespread circulation by the outbreak of the war. Here a nurse in a London hospital practises the gas drill. After the horrors of the mustard and chlorine gas attacks on the battlefields of the First World War, the threat of gas attack seemed very real and was utterly terrifying. It was essential that mothers with young babies were practised in the quick application of the gas mask to avoid the slightest chance of contamination. *(IWM D 651)*

The perceived threat of gas attack was such that the government encouraged the public to wear their gas masks for 15 minutes each day to get used to them. At the beginning of the war it was an offence to leave the house without your gas mask, and citizens were supposed to carry it at all times. However, the lack of action during the Phoney War meant that the fervour with which people carried their gas masks waned. Here, a couple relax in front of the fire during their 15-minute practice! *(IWM D 3948)*

ARP wardens were seen by many as figures of fun, and this photograph showing wardens wearing their gas masks while off-duty at an ARP post does little to contradict this view. However, if a gas attack had taken place, the help of the hundreds of thousands of people working (mostly on a voluntary basis) in Civil Defence would have been essential. (IWM D 3898)

played their part. The Air Raid Wardens Service was set up in April 1937 and had recruited 200,000 members by the middle of 1938. ARP staff were responsible for everything connected with a possible enemy attack, from the initial detection of bombs and fire-watching, through the rescue of people trapped in the rubble of bombed-out buildings, to the clear-up operations needed to return the cities to some form of normality.

Inextricably linked to the ARP was the work of the WVS and other such organisations to provide refreshments, both to air raid casualties and to Civil Defence workers. This cooperation continued well after the war into the 1960s, when Civil Defence was still an important issue.

The fire services were essential during the Blitz, and went through several changes during the war years. At the beginning of the war the fire services consisted of a combination of the professional firemen of the London Fire Brigade and other local services (of which there were 1,600 across the UK) and the 23,000 auxiliaries who were called up at the start of the war. The AFS (Auxiliary Fire Service) was created in 1938. Although its numbers were originally disappointingly low, it played a hugely important part in dealing with the aftermath of the Blitz. In 1941 the National Fire Service

Auxiliary Fire Servicemen Richard Southern and R.H. Betts fight a fire among rubble somewhere in London. The AFS played a huge part in assisting the existing professional fire services across the country, and nowhere more so than in London. Conflict between the auxiliaries and the professionals led to the creation of the National Fire Service (NFS) in 1941. *(IWM D 2650)*

Sydney Collingsworth (centre) and his NFS colleagues play cards between 'shouts' at a fire station in London, c. 1943. The poster above Sydney's head is advertising a Fire Service dance to be held at Hornsey Town Hall. (IWM D 12055)

A fire engine leaves Fulham fire station on a training exercise, c. 1943. This drill enabled firecrews, members of the ARP and rescue squads to work alongside medical crews and perfect their roles in case of a genuine incident. *(IWM D 7888)*

(NFS) was formed in an attempt to unify all the disparate services in order to face any onslaught of German bombs with professionalism and coordination. In addition to the differences between the professional and auxiliary bodies, the various professional agencies had major differences in structure and this, coupled with the technical differences in the equipment used, led to confusion when these services were called upon to work together. The NFS continued until the Fire Service Bill of 1947 transferred responsibility back to the individual local authorities. The 147 fire brigades were denationalised in April 1948.

The Home Guard was another hugely important part of civil defence. Originally formed as the Local Defence Volunteers (LDV) in May 1940, the Home Guard (the name was changed in July 1940, on Churchill's insistence) aimed to provide an efficient defence force against an enemy invader and to free up members of the regular army for training. Some 250,000 men had registered within 24 hours and by the time the name had changed there were over 1.5 million members. The stereotypical 'Dad's Army' view of the Home Guard is reflected in the official photographs; the original uniform consisted solely of a brassard (arm band) featuring the initials LDV (and later HG). However, from August 1940 Home Guard units were allied to county regiments, and by the end of February 1941 the amateurish slant was removed, following the establishment of a formal rank system and the introduction of conscription which ended the voluntary nature of the Home Guard.

From 1942 members of the Home Guard were given basic Civil Defence training and also served in anti-aircraft batteries (both in batteries manned solely by Home Guard personnel and in mixed batteries alongside members of the Auxiliary Territorial Service (ATS)), thus freeing up more army personnel for training and overseas fighting. This flexible approach to the Home Guard meant that it was able to contribute to all aspects of Civil Defence in Britain.

Civil Defence as an organisation was, to all intents and purposes, disbanded in September 1944, with many Civil Defence measures being relaxed, although it continued in a different form until the late 1960s. A large stand-down parade was held for the Home Guard on 2 December 1944.

Although perhaps regarded now (and occasionally at the time) as a bit of a joke, an amateurish band of 'do-gooding' civilians playing at war, it is clear that members of the various Civil Defence organisations and the Home Guard did much to defend Britain during the Second World War. Although the feared German invasion never came (indeed, it is debatable whether such an invasion could have

This photograph, showing a Home Guard charge in Springfield, Essex, in 1941, gives a rather 'Dad's Army' view of this organisation. However, by this time the Home Guard had proper uniforms and ranks, and units were affiliated to regular army regiments. The Home Guard's main role was to guard its local area, but it also worked with ATS units to man anti-aircraft guns. (IWM D 4259)

The ability to distinguish between allied and enemy aircraft during a threatened invasion was of the utmost importance and training was essential. Here members of the Home Guard are schooled in aircraft recognition in 1943. Much of this training was led by members of the women's services. *(IWM D 12232)*

Home Guard bayonet instructor Cpl George Batchelor examines his bayonet before a training exercise. Cpl Batchelor, a window cleaner by trade, had been an under-age soldier during the First World War and served on the North-West Frontier in India. *(IWM D 9264)*

been successfully repelled), the psychological effect on the civilian population, who knew that a network of Civil Defence cells existed, shouldn't be underplayed. Indeed, by joining Civil Defence people were able to contribute to the war effort simply by maintaining morale. Civil Defence organisations also did much to help victims of air raids. Their efforts to rescue, and provide support for, those affected by air raids, as well as the invaluable work they did in fire-watching, certainly prevented many deaths and further damage to property from enemy bombs.

A roof-spotter carries out his fire-watching
duty from a London roof, c. 1941. It was
imperative that any sign of fire was
extinguished immediately to prevent it
spreading to adjoining buildings. Fire-watching
rotas were drawn up and everyone took their
turn on the rooftops. Every large commercial
building was obliged by law to implement
a system of fire-watching.
(IWM D 4603)

Although they were not strictly part of the MoI, various surveys were conducted during the war on behalf of many different organisations, including Mass Observation, which began in 1938. Here, surveyor Mrs Margaret Thomas interviews Mrs Cohen on her doorstep in Stepney, on behalf of the Board of Trade, 'who want to know whether selected commodities are in short supply in different areas'. *(IWM D 18835)*

CHAPTER 5

THE PROPAGANDA MACHINE

THE ROLE OF THE

MINISTRY OF INFORMATION

All the information that reached the public regarding the war on its various fronts (including at home) and the various war effort campaigns (such as salvage drives, fuel economy and 'Dig for Victory') were coordinated via the MoI, and the posters and exhibitions designed by them to promote such campaigns provide a good insight into the mindset of the time.

The idea of a Ministry of Information was first discussed in October 1935, when a sub-committee of the Committee of Imperial Defence was formed to consider the issue. The First World War had seen a number of separate agencies performing the various tasks of the MoI (although an information ministry of sorts was created under Lord Beaverbrook in 1918), and it was felt that one individual body was needed to coordinate the dissemination of information during wartime. The purpose of the MoI, as prepared in 1936, was to present the national case both overseas and on the Home Front, and involved the production of propaganda and the preservation of civilian morale. The latter was extremely important during the Second World War, as it was imperative that the public remained fully behind the war effort in order for it to succeed. In this way, then, the importance of the MoI is clear.

The Ministry was divided up into five main sections, dealing with news, control (censorship), publicity, administration and collecting

(intelligence gathering). The first Minister of Information was Lord Macmillan. The Ministry went through three ministers, including Sir John Reith and Duff Cooper, and numerous alterations to its structure before the arrival of Brendan Bracken in July 1941 settled the situation.

The Photographs Division, which created and compiled the 'D Series' on which this book is based, was formed in May 1940 to gather all photographic material relating to the war at home and overseas. These photographs would be censored and distributed as the MoI saw fit, particularly for use as propaganda on the Home Front and abroad, mainly in the United States. Although the division's main job was to compile photographs taken by press photographers (both at home and overseas) and official military photographers on the various fronts, there were some special MoI commissions, such as that of Bill Brandt in 1940 who was asked to take photographs of shelterers in the London Underground. Cecil Beaton was also employed as an MoI 'Special Photographer'. Both Brandt and Beaton were hugely important photographers before their commission by the MoI and continued to be influential in their field after the war. Later still, in 1944, five photographers were appointed as official MoI photographers to further the photographic coverage of the Home Front, leading to a much more proactive approach by the MoI.

The main role of the Ministry of Information was, of course, to tell the public about the war and to inform them of events in the various parts of the world in which the Army, Navy and Air Force were fighting. In addition, a key task was to keep up public morale and encourage people to contribute to the war effort in any way that they could. The main way in which these tasks were tackled was through the production of posters, leaflets and exhibitions, highlighting, among other things, particular military achievements or home security issues.

The 'D Series' photographs are very wide-ranging in their coverage of Home Front life, and also give us an excellent idea of the workings of the MoI itself. The 'D Series' is unique in that it not only includes pictures taken for use in exhibitions, on posters or in pamphlets focusing on a specific MoI campaign, but also contains photographs of the exhibitions themselves, showing how the original photographs were actually used. There are many examples of this in the 'D Series', and in the following pages a few of them are highlighted, as they also illustrate some of the main themes that ran through the Second World War.

Civil servants at work in the offices of the MoI Photograph Division in November 1941. Initially, the job of the Division was to collate all photographs taken by official and agency photographers and to make sure that their self-censorship was correctly implemented. They then distributed this material to various bodies, including the MoI's own publicity and news sections. *(IWM D 5210)*

The D series contains a mixture of photographs taken for exhibitions, publications and leaflets, and photographs of the exhibitions themselves, each based on a particular theme. These two photographs are a good example of this, focusing on preventing the wastage of bread. 'Bread into Battle' was an exhibition held at Charing Cross in June 1942, which encouraged the public to use every last scrap of bread, even baking it again into biscuits, and to buy National Loaf, in order that less grain would have to be transported by the vulnerable merchant convoys. *(IWM D 8374/D 8723)*

In addition to the production of exhibitions, particularly at Charing Cross station and on the bombed John Lewis department store site on Oxford Street, the MoI also had a display van that travelled around to various locations. Exhibitions were frequently changed and related to whichever aspect of the war effort was being promoted at that time.

Most MoI campaigns revolved around the ideas of the reduction of waste, the reuse of everything and, to a certain extent, self-sufficiency (particularly with regard to food), both of the individual and of Britain. Characters such as 'Mrs Sew-and-Sew' and 'Private Scrap' (created by the Board of Trade) explained how materials could be salvaged and reused, and the Ministry of Food's 'Dr Carrot' and 'Potato Pete' encouraged people to grow and eat fresh vegetables. Fuel economy and salvage became part of everyday life, with pig bins in place for food scraps and sewing and dressmaking classes available to help people make the most of their existing wardrobes. Other MoI campaigns revolved around the ARP, the implementation of the blackout and the wearing of gas masks. They also promoted the idea of good health and its link to the success of the war effort.

Not all exhibitions were issue- or campaign-based, as this large format exhibition in Brighton demonstrates. The aim of this event was to recruit more women into the Auxiliary Territorial Service (ATS), tempting them with room sets illustrating typical sleeping quarters, mess rooms and the type of work in which ATS members were engaged. *(IWM D 5411)*

Opposite and above: An aspect of Home Front life about which the MoI was keen to raise awareness, particularly during the early years of the war, was the threat of gas attack. The gas mask was a fundamental part of protection against gas, but this exhibition, entitled 'Poison Gas' (held at Charing Cross in August/September 1941), highlighted other aspects of gas protection and the work of ARP crews in the event of such an attack. The exhibition explained how a gas mask was constructed and advised the public on what they should do if they were splashed with blister gas. Also highlighted was the work of gas cleansing stations where citizens would go for decontaminating showers and first aid. *(IWM D 3492/D 4195)*

'Army' was the largest MoI travelling exhibition, seen here on the bombed John Lewis site in London. This exhibition travelled around the country and explained the work of the Army both overseas and in the UK, highlighting things such as the equipment used and the way in which a field kitchen functioned, and included photographs of the most recent overseas campaigns. *(IWM D 15150)*

"PUT BOOKS IN
THE FORCES BLITZED LIBRAR
PRIVATE SCRAP'S IN TOWN
. . . COME AND MEET HIM

Many venues, including a space at Charing Cross station, various town halls across the country and numerous shops, were commandeered by the MoI for use as exhibition spaces. However, even these were not enough and mobile exhibition vans were also used to take the current exhibition campaign to those areas that did not have suitable spaces. This van carried the 'Private Scrap' exhibition, illustrating the importance of salvage and recycling in the conservation of limited raw materials such as rubber and various metals. *(IWM D 13549)*

Promoting good health was a key issue for the MoI. This exhibition at Charing Cross advised the public on healthy eating, the prevention of illness and the importance of exercise, and linked health with the success of the war effort. According to the exhibition, 20 million days (or 3,500 tanks, 1,000 bombers and 1 million rifles) were lost to the war effort each year through workers getting colds or flu. (IWM D 11947)

Photographs of the exhibitions are very interesting as they are a real reflection of the time, giving us an idea of the topics relevant to the period, the design aspect of the exhibitions, the types of people that visited them, the British population's thirst for information about all aspects of the war (illustrated by the numbers of people in attendance), and in particular the views held by the MoI, and what they felt was important for people to know (or not know) about the course of the war and the progress of the war effort. Topics such as 'Make Do and Mend', salvage, agriculture and food production, fuel economy, National Savings and Civil Defence crop up time and again in the 'D Series', both in the photographs themselves and in the photographs of the exhibitions. This highlights the few key areas that were of particular importance to both the Ministry and the public, giving us a real insight into the minds of those living through the Second World War.

As well as photographs and display panels highlighting war work, some exhibitions had people on show too. The aim of this women war workers exhibition in Bristol was to encourage women not currently engaged on war work to get involved. The exhibits included women demonstrating various pieces of manufacturing equipment and the production of fuses and cables. *(IWM D 10852)*

A British soldier advises two GIs at the British Army School of Hygiene, c. 1943. The BASH aimed to promote army efficiency by maintaining the health of the troops through good hygiene. According to the original MoI caption, over 85,000 men had trained at BASH since the outbreak of the war. The close contact between US and British troops on the battlefield meant that it was important that each army was familiar with the methods of the other. *(IWM D 19481)*

CHAPTER 6

THE ARMED
FORCES ON THE
HOME FRONT

One of the most significant changes on the Home Front during the Second World War was the appearance of armed forces personnel on the streets of Britain's cities and villages, in particular those from overseas. Although the greatest numbers of service personnel crowded into Britain in preparation for the D-Day landings in 1944, huge numbers of soldiers, sailors and airmen (including those from Poland, France, Norway, Canada, Australia, the West Indies, Africa and, of course, the United States) were stationed in the UK throughout the later war years and became a common sight in the towns and villages of the British Isles from 1941 to 1942. Indeed, Canadian troops began arriving in the UK in 1939, with 7,500 reaching Britain on 17 December that year. Although predominantly male, this influx also included women in the associated auxiliary services.

Training was the main reason for the flood of troops into the UK, not only for the campaigns in North Africa and Italy but also, later, in preparation for the invasion of France in June 1944. In addition to battle training, the troops learned fieldcraft (that is, how to survive in the field). Thousands of troops passed through Britain on their way from the United States to Europe, and the UK was also a place to recuperate after fighting at the front. Other soldiers were actively engaged on anti-aircraft work, supported largely by the ATS and also by some Home Guard units.

The widespread conscription of men (from 3 September 1939) and women (from 1 December 1941) into the services during the

The sheer number of service personnel who found themselves on British soil at some time or other during the Second World War is illustrated by this services accommodation noticeboard at Glasgow railway station. Here a group of naval personnel consult the board to decide where they will stay for the night. *(IWM D 18783)*

'people's war' influenced the nature of the training received by troops on the Home Front, particularly with regard to the Army. An ACI (Army Council Instruction) in November 1940 stated that it was no longer necessary to polish everything in sight, and advised that items that would be used on the battlefield should be kept clean but allowed to become dull. Such ACIs, although ignored by some, aimed to modernise the Army and adapt it for modern warfare. There was also a lot less drill and an increase in more useful battlefield training.

Britain provided an excellent training ground for the Royal Navy (RN), which made the most of the numerous shore stations across the country. Naval training was essential, and the RN played a huge part in the Battle of the Atlantic in 1941, providing escorts for the vulnerable merchant ships carrying goods from Canada and the United States. One of the most difficult problems for the Royal Navy was the German U-Boats, which had sunk HMS *Royal Oak* at Scapa Flow in the Orkneys in 1939. The Navy countered this menace by introducing new and improved anti-submarine measures. The majority of naval personnel were, however, on active service overseas, and only stayed in Britain for their initial training and while on leave. Most of the 'at home' tasks of the Royal Navy were carried out by the Women's Royal Naval Service (see p. 106).

The importance of the Royal Air Force (RAF) was clearly seen during the Battle of Britain (10 July–31 October 1940). Although the RAF lost approximately 790 aircraft during the battle, compared with German losses of roughly 1,389 aircraft (exact numbers vary between sources), the RAF's fighter squadrons successfully denied the *Luftwaffe* air superiority. RAF squadrons included Australian, Canadian, Czech, Free French, Indian and West Indian pilots and aircrew, and, even before the official entry of the US into the war after the Japanese attack on Pearl Harbor in December 1941, many Americans volunteered to serve in Eagle Squadrons in the RAF. Later in the war the United States Army Air Force (USAAF) served at air bases in the UK, predominantly in East Anglia.

At the beginning of the war the RAF was not in good shape, with only 1,421 airfields, 1,911 aircraft, 20,033 aircrew and 153,925 groundcrew. These figures gradually increased throughout the course of the war, and by 1945 aircraft numbers had swelled to 9,000, aircrew to 185,595, and groundcrew to 865,517, including those from the Dominions. The RAF actively sought personnel from other Commonwealth countries, and by the end of the war a total of over 17,500 men and women from across the Commonwealth had volunteered to serve in the RAF. Aircraft of Bomber Command

Physical training Dutch-style! According to the original MoI caption, Dutch PT was 'unusually energetic' and 'leapfrog and other games' featured highly in their training. One of the most important aspects of the war was that it led to the influx of service personnel of all nationalities. Many Allied soldiers, sailors and airmen married British women and set up home in the UK. *(IWM D 2194)*

A Newfoundland soldier is instructed in rifle shooting by British Sgt Lou Newbury in 1942. Canadian troops were the first to arrive in Britain, with the first 7,500 reaching British shores on 17 December 1939. During the course of the war 335,000 Canadians came to Britain, many of whom helped to train, and trained with, Home Guard units. *(IWM D 8904)*

Opposite: Sailors at HMS *Western Isles* learn to hunt U-Boats in 1944. All the training given here was based on lessons learned from the Battle of the Atlantic, and live ammunition was used to make the training as realistic as possible. According to the original caption: 'This submarine has surfaced near a frigate that had been "hunting" her and attacking for more than two hours – typical of actual experience in the war against the U-Boats.' *(IWM D 20266)*

Above: Ratings on this Royal Navy destroyer slept in hammocks and were awakened with the traditional cries of 'heave-ho, heave-ho, lash up and stow' and 'show a leg, show a leg or the Purser's stocking'. The latter saying dates back to a time when sailors' wives were allowed on board, and a stockinged leg dangling outside the hammock would indicate that the occupant was female and thus entitled to an extra half-hour's sleep! *(IWM D 16130)*

The Merchant Navy was of huge importance to the war effort, transporting essential goods to Britain. West Indian, Maltese, Polish and Indian merchant seamen, to name but a few, all contributed to the success of the Merchant Navy. Many Merchant Navy hostels were established in Britain during the war, including West Indies House in Newcastle upon Tyne, shown here.
(IWM D 5762)

A bomber crew is briefed before setting out on a mission, *c.* 1941. RAF Bomber Command, led first by ACM Sir Charles Portal and ACM Sir Sholto Douglas and from 23 February 1942 by Sir Arthur 'Bomber' Harris, carried out both day and night raids across Germany, in an attempt to wear down the morale of civilians. It also targeted U-Boat pens and other German war industry. *(IWM D 6015)*

frequently flew dangerous missions to bomb various targets in Germany while Coastal Command provided air support to the merchant ships and Royal Navy vessels circling British shores.

Perhaps the most striking aspect of the armed forces in the Second World War was the sheer diversity of nationalities, accents and races that appeared on Britain's shores. By 1944 there were 1,421,000 Allied, Dominion and Colonial troops based in the UK. However, although men and women of many countries were billeted in Britain, it was arguably the Americans that had the greatest impact. The GIs (so-named because all their equipment was stamped Government Issue) began to arrive in January 1942, and reached a peak of 1,526,965 in May 1944. Regarded by many as a tonic, the Americans brought a sense of excitement, Hollywood glamour and morale-boosting items (such as nylon stockings and chocolate) to a heavily rationed Britain, although many British citizens disliked the strong US presence. US aid to Britain had begun long before its official entry into the war, with the Lend-Lease scheme allowing Roosevelt to 'lend' equipment and food to Britain while technically remaining neutral (although there was no intention of payment ever being made). Indeed, the United States introduced conscription in 1940, despite the fact that it was not yet at war. The US Army on all fronts reached a peak of 8.3 million men in 1945, 7 million of whom had been drafted.

West Indian volunteers to the RAF on parade, c. 1944. The event was attended by the Secretary of State for the Colonies, the Rt Hon. Col Oliver Stanley MC, MP, and AM Sir Arthur Barrett KCB, the Air Officer Commanding Technical Training Command. In total, more than 6,000 West Indians were recruited into the RAF between 1943 and 1945, with 5,500 serving as groundcrew and over 700 training as aircrew. (IWM D 21139)

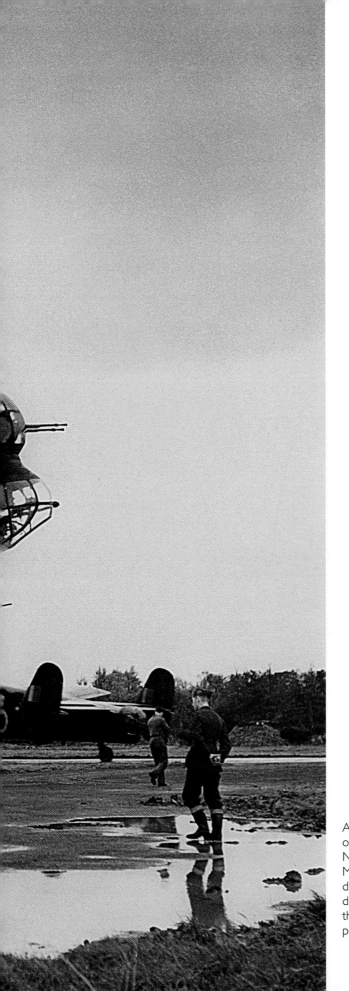

A Halifax II of 35 Squadron prepares for take-off from Linton-on-Ouse in October 1941. A training unit until its reformation in November 1940, 35 Squadron flew its first Halifax mission in March 1941. Halifax bombers were constructed by many different firms, with the designers Handley Page supplying drawings to various 'daughter companies'. In addition, some of the floors for Halifaxes were actually built, among other aircraft parts, by the football pools firm Littlewoods. *(IWM D 6054)*

Before the United States entered the war after the Japanese attack on Pearl Harbor in 1941, some Americans joined the RAF in Eagle Squadrons. Here we see Flg Off Barry Mehan (left) and Flt Lt S.R. Edner, both from California, scrambling into action after receiving a message that enemy aircraft were approaching. (IWM D 9521)

Above: Pte Julian Desrosiers serves Sgt William Luman at the London Post Exchange. Such shops were provided for American servicemen in Britain as reciprocal aid (a sort of reverse Lend-Lease). PXs, as they were known, provided GIs with cigarettes, candy and other items, which not only reminded them of home but also made them popular with British women and children – many things rationed in Britain were freely available in the United States. *(IWM D 11825)*

Opposite: Sgt Bert Spence from Crookston, Minnesota, teaches Edwin Aylott the finer points of baseball in the village of Burton Bradstock in Dorset, 1944. American troops were billeted across the UK, and although their camps were closed establishments the soldiers did try to integrate themselves into the local community; some might say that the numbers of relationships between GIs and British women indicated a little too much integration. *(IWM D 20152)*

The original MoI caption for this photograph reads: 'In a Naafi, Patience "Pat" Parr, of Taunton, Somerset, takes a dollar bill from a US soldier, gives him four shillings and ten pence in exchange.' The Navy, Army and Air Force Institution canteens provided a place for GIs and British troops to relax, and enabled GIs to get to grips with British money, which was totally different from the American decimal system. *(IWM D 17225)*

Perhaps the most important issue of the Second World War with regard to the armed forces was the increased numbers of women involved. Huge numbers of women joined the auxiliary forces, and these played a much greater role than they had done in the First World War. The ATS started life on a voluntary basis in 1938 and was given full military status in 1941. Conscription for women into the ATS began in 1942. By mid-1943, when peak strength was reached, the ATS had 210,308 members. All types of non-combatant duties were carried out by the ATS, from clerks and drivers, to working with the Home Guard and regular army units on anti-aircraft sites. Initially the ATS also provided support to the RAF, but the Women's Auxiliary Air Force (WAAF) was formed in 1939 to take over this role. By the end of the war the WAAF had 182,000 members. Again, the main duties for WAAFs were as drivers, cooks or clerks, but many also manned barrage balloon winches. Many WAAFs also trained members of the Home Guard in aircraft recognition, essential should the feared invasion ever come.

The Women's Royal Naval Service (WRNS) first recruited volunteers in 1939. Unlike the ATS and the WAAF, the WRNS was seen as an integral part of the Royal Navy and its members were never known as auxiliaries. Duties ranged from jobs as clerks and cooks to working in the postal service, as messengers, and in the training of sailors.

Clearly, then, it was the norm to see men and women in uniform on Britain's streets. Many of those billeted in the UK from overseas stayed here after the war, creating new lives for themselves with British wives. Likewise, many women married GIs and moved to the United States. Undoubtedly the influx of troops into Britain had a far-reaching impact on the lives not only of those who fought, and those upon whom these troops were billeted, but also on the make-up of certain areas of Britain: even today there is a strong Polish connection with Scotland.

Right: Although not permitted to fire the guns, members of the ATS were crucial to the success of anti-aircraft gun sites across Britain during the Second World War. This ATS member is working as a spotter, looking out for any sign of enemy aircraft, at an anti-aircraft site in 1942. *(IWM D 8307)*

Below: This photograph is part of an MoI sequence entitled 'The Unknown Girl behind the Sea Battle', which followed 'Wren Unknown' in her work. Here 'Wren Unknown' (second from right) manoeuvres ships in the Operations Room. Many members of the WRNS were employed in roles such as this, and were vital in keeping an accurate up-to-date picture of naval positions in battle. *(IWM D 7289)*

ATS Sgt Chamberlen (aged 21) and Pte Bartels (aged 19) at work on mirror range-finders. The women watched for shell bursts in the sky and then marked the position of the bursts on the mirror. This position was then transferred on to special paper in the Observation Post room. Comparison of the readings taken at several posts allowed an accurate reading of the actual shell bursts to be obtained. *(IWM D 12701)*

A WAAF driver collects members of an RAF Wellington bomber crew from their dispersal points to take them to the debriefing. WAAFs provided tremendous support to the RAF in many roles, with over 64,000 women being employed as officers and other ranks by 1940. *(IWM D 10849)*

ACW/2 Norah mans a theodolite at the Meteorological Training Centre in London. Behind her a fellow WAAF examines a weather balloon. Weather conditions greatly affected the success of RAF missions, and the work of WAAFs in meteorology was therefore essential.
(IWM D 1118)

Overseas, particularly US, assistance was not just limited to service personnel, as these women of the Anglo-American Ambulance Unit illustrate. Here we see (left to right) Mrs Dale, Mrs Beaven, Miss Thomas and Miss Hedley rushing to their stations somewhere in the Northern Region, where they were helping the Civil Medical Authorities. *(IWM D 3996)*

Opposite: Wrens were employed in any number of diverse trades and here we see 'Wrens with the Fleet Mail' at work at a 'South-Eastern Port'. According to the original caption, this group of Wrens dealt with a daily average of 7,000 letters and 300 parcels. The mail-boat was hugely important for the morale of sailors, bringing news of home. *(IWM D 22596)*

The ubiquitous ration book and clothing ration book. Most items of food could not be bought without the ration book, and once your week's rations were purchased no more could be bought until the following week. Clothing was also rationed from 1 June 1941, with each item being given a points value. The basic clothes ration for adults was at first 66 coupons per year (although this was later reduced to 60 coupons): a coat cost 13 coupons, a pair of trousers 8 coupons and a dress 11 coupons plus the price. *(IWM D 1131)*

CHAPTER 7

FOOD, FASHION
AND FURNISHINGS

Food production, highlighted by campaigns such as 'Dig For Victory', held particular importance during the war. Merchant shipping convoys were frequently attacked and were under pressure to focus on the transportation of munitions and food for troops, which were naturally regarded as more important than civilian meals. So, despite resistance from various quarters, rationing was introduced in January 1940 in an attempt to control the limited food supplies available.

Initially, scientists working on behalf of the War Cabinet devised the 'Basal Diet', which was the absolute minimum of food on which an individual could survive. However, although the volunteers testing this diet suffered no ill-effects, it was decided that it was too harsh a menu, and the idea was shelved. But basic foodstuffs such as butter, bacon, cheese, milk and tea were rationed, and the ingredients used to bake bread were altered, transforming it into the 'National Loaf'. However, one of the ironies of rationing was that the bacon ration was set higher than the average level of consumption before the war. Indeed, many people were actually healthier at the end of the war than they had been in 1939, owing to the eating of more vegetables and less fat and sugar.

Fruit and vegetables were never rationed, and the consumption of fresh produce was vigorously encouraged. Lord Woolton, the Minister of Food, after whom the 'Woolton Pie' was named ('steak and kidney pie without the steak and kidney'), passionately advocated the use of potatoes and carrots (abundantly available on allotments up and down the country) in every recipe.

Although eating out had always been popular with the higher echelons in Britain, it became even more so during the Second

The official MoI caption for this photograph reads: 'Rations mean headaches for Wynnstay's hostess Mrs Minnie Murless. Every two months full detailed lists, down to cups of tea, must be sent to the Food Office; every week forms for butcher, grocer [must be completed]; permits must be sought for coal, paraffin and food for cow, hens, pigs. Mrs Murless, hostess, clips coupons from ration books of guests staying over five days.' *(IWM D 18488)*

Queues were a common sight in wartime Britain.
Housewives would register with a particular retailer and
often had to queue in order to collect their rations.
As queuing was such a large part of shopping, and took up
a great deal of time, members of the WVS and other
organisations often went shopping on behalf of those women
engaged in war work, thus preventing them from missing out on any
new deliveries of unrationed foods, such as fish. (IWM D 25037)

Staff set the tables at the Martinez Restaurant in Swallow Street, London, c. 1940. Despite the shortages and the imposition of Austerity rules on meals, restaurants such as this did a roaring trade during the war, providing some form of escape from coupon counting and potato pie. Although the Austerity regulations made for simpler, less elaborate meals, it is still very easy to see the difference between luxury restaurants and the later purely functional British Restaurants.
(IWM D 8371)

World War as restaurant meals were 'off-ration': any food consumed out of the house was additional to the weekly rations received. The use of ration books in restaurants was discussed, but it was felt that the administration of such a scheme would be disastrously complicated. In order to make things fairer (the wealthy could eat out regularly, while still receiving the same rations as everyone else), guidelines were introduced whereby only three courses could be served, food was simpler and a maximum price was fixed. 'Victory V' meals symbolised the fight for victory through food: appetising and nutritious, they saved on shipping as they consisted mainly of home-grown produce.

Originally set up to provide meals for those who had been bombed-out, British Restaurants aimed to provide hot, healthy and cheap meals for the public in comfortable and attractive surroundings. As well as providing emergency meals, these British Restaurants became a way for the Ministry of Food to improve the nutritional intake of the population.

In November 1940 it became compulsory for factories with 250 or more workers doing some form of war work to provide canteen facilities. There were two categories of industrial canteens: one for

heavy industries and another for the smaller ones. Miners, steel workers and other manual workers were given extra rations, particularly of American Lend-Lease cheese. School meals were another way for the authorities to ensure that people were eating correctly, and extra milk was provided for children.

Emergency feeding was hugely important, with the WVS and the Queen's Messenger Flying Food Convoys providing food in the immediate aftermath of an air raid. The YWCA and Salvation Army also operated emergency canteens, and emergency meal centres were set up in larger towns in February 1941 to provide food for those whose cooking facilities had been damaged or destroyed during air raids.

The main development in fashion and clothing production during the Second World War was the Utility scheme. Adopted in 1941, the scheme was an attempt by the government to control the raw materials used in clothing manufacture and to limit the amount of fabric used in the production of garments, in order to conserve these scarce materials. To qualify as Utility, items had to be made from controlled materials and be licensed by the government. The Utility scheme provided benefits for the government, manufacturers and consumers alike: the government was able to conserve raw materials,

Eating out was hugely popular during the Second World War, and nowhere more so than in the chain of Lyons' Corner Houses. Here we see customers at the Lyons' Brasserie Corner House in London's Coventry Street enjoying a spot of afternoon tea, c. 1941. (IWM D 6573)

Although initially created as emergency feeding centres, British Restaurants were very popular places, providing well-balanced, healthy and cheap off-ration meals: between 60 and 70 per cent of those surveyed by the British Institute of Public Opinion in 1942 and again in 1944 stated that they would like to see British Restaurants continuing after the war. Many British Restaurants reused buildings (including an old henhouse in Nottingham), although eventually prefabs were supplied which could be erected quickly on any available vacant site. This British Restaurant in Woolmore Road reused an old school building. *(IWM D 10681)*

manufacturers who signed up for the scheme were guaranteed a certain amount of the available raw materials, and the public benefited from well-designed, good-quality goods. Initially, there was scepticism about the Utility scheme, as people feared that some form of civilian uniform would be introduced, but overall the reception was good and the Board of Trade invited ten designers (including Norman Hartnell and Hardy Amies) from the Incorporated Society of London Fashion Designers to create a selection of outfits for Utility production.

In addition to the Utility restrictions, clothing was also subject to a set of regulations known as Austerity. Austerity items were not necessarily made from Utility fabrics, but aimed to reduce excess decoration, trimmings and the use of surplus fabric, again to conserve raw materials. The aim was to make clothing simpler, and with no (or at least a lot less) frills. Austerity was a design style whereas Utility was more holistic, as restrictions were in place from the initial design and creation of the fabric to the final garment.

All Utility items were marked with the distinctive Board of Trade Utility stamp CC41, which derived from the words Civilian Clothing and the year of its inception, 1941. This stamp continued to be used as the symbol of Utility, being put on all sorts of items that were clearly not Civilian Clothing.

Girls of Baldock County Council School in Hertfordshire enjoy their morning milk, 1944. Free or cheap milk was an important part of life for children during the war, and it was a good way for the Ministry of Food to ensure that children got the vitamins and minerals they needed. Provision of milk in schools had existed before the war, but it was extended to cater for more children as time went by. *(IWM D 20552)*

Above and opposite: The 'D Series' contains many examples of the designs put forward by members of the Incorporated Society of Fashion Designers to the Board of Trade as part of the attempt to encourage the production of fashionable Utility garments, which looked good despite the restrictions. These photographs show Molyneux's original design for a striking women's suit in a checked tartan pattern, and the same design being worn by a model (right) before being put into production. The addition of a dark-coloured blouse and sharply angled hat complete the look. *(IWM D 9873 / D 9654)*

Indeed, Utility was gradually extended to include furniture, crockery and soft furnishings, and items such as clothing (which had been rationed since 1941) were given a coupon value. Utility furniture was developed from Standard Emergency Furniture, a range created in February 1941 for people who had been bombed-out of their homes. Newly-weds and bombed-out people received extra coupons towards Utility furniture, and the purchase of second-hand furniture was encouraged. Emphasis was placed on simplicity of design and mass production, but also on quality; these items were built to last, and the irony is that many people were able to obtain much better quality furniture during the war than they had done before! The Utility scheme continued after the war, lasting until 21 January 1953.

It is clear that the health and outlook of civilians during the war was fundamentally changed by the shortages of food, clothing and furnishings. People may have had to struggle with coupon values, and with scraping together enough dried egg and sugar to make a birthday cake, but at the end of it all they were healthier and had long-lasting, good-quality clothes and furniture which are the epitome of the 1940s.

Opposite: This grey crêpe dinner dress shows that wartime clothing could still be extremely glamorous and chic, despite (as in this case) the imposition of Austerity rules. *(IWM D 14824)*

Above: The blackout was softened for fashion-conscious women by the sale of luminous flowers, which were both attractive and practical. Such flowers were preferable to the armbands or alternative button badges, adding a touch of glamour. *(IWM D 73)*

Turbans and hairnets were the order of the day during the war, both to comply with factory rules and also to cover up hair that was suffering from a lack of cosmetics and shampoos. The shortage of hair products meant that a visit to the hairdresser could be expensive, despite the fact that, among other things, dyes were heavily diluted! Here actress Diana Wynyard visits hairdresser Mr Steiner at his salon in Grosvenor Street in 1944. The salon was in a basement previously used as a public air raid shelter. *(IWM D 18214)*

In addition to clothing, crockery and other furnishings, Utility regulations also applied to furniture. This room set is part of an exhibition held at the Building Centre in 1942, which aimed to encourage people to buy Utility furniture. The exhibition was opened by Hugh Dalton, the President of the Board of Trade. There were several designs of furniture, and priority was given to newly-weds and those who were rebuilding their homes after air raids. Discounts were also given to those purchasing second-hand furniture. (IWM D 11051)

Left: The rules and style of Utility were not confined to clothing and furniture. This display of crockery shows the simplicity and versatility of Utility crockery (most of which was used by caterers in British Restaurants). For example, the lid from the teapot could be used with the handle-less cup to create a jam-pot. (IWM D 11123)

CHAPTER 8

SUFFER THE LITTLE ONES

THE EXPERIENCES OF CHILDREN ON THE HOME FRONT

Photographs of young children lining railway platforms with gas masks and luggage labels round their necks provide some of the most enduring and iconic images of the Second World War. Although perhaps the most significant event in the lives of children during this period, there *was* more to their experience of the Second World War than just as evacuees.

Plans for the evacuation of children, pregnant women and the disabled from danger areas had been discussed as early as 1931, when a sub-committee of the Imperial Defence Committee was set up to discuss the issue, with a secret report being published in 1934. Despite this, discussion over who should fund it was still going on as late as 1938. The mammoth task of moving the evacuees (whose numbers were originally estimated at 3 million) fell to the Ministry of Health led by Walter Elliott (who served as Minister of Health between May 1938 and May 1940), and the country was divided up into three distinct zones: danger areas, neutral areas and reception areas.

The government encouraged people to disperse, fearing that a concentration of people in one place would lead to higher casualties. This idea went against the theories of gas warfare expert Professor J.B.S. Haldane, who believed that the concentration or dispersal of

Although many schools were evacuated during the war, some chose to remain in London and adapted their practices to take air raids into account. At Greek Road School in south-east London this cellar or basement was commandeered for use as a classroom.
(IWM D 3161)

Evacuees from Bristol, with luggage labels, suitcases and gas masks, arriving at Kingsbridge in 1941. It is interesting to note the different facial expressions of these children: some are happy and excited, enjoying the adventure, while others look quite worried about the whole thing, summing up the mixed emotions felt by evacuees across the country. *(IWM D 2593)*

Education and billeting officers check their paperwork ready for the arrival of evacuees to Kingsbridge from Bristol in 1941. Billeting officers had a particularly difficult task, and stories abound of the failure of such officers to match householders to appropriate evacuees. Looking back, however, one cannot fail to be impressed by the phenomenal degree of organisation that went into the evacuation programme.
(IWM D 2589)

people would have no bearing on the effectiveness of bombs. Another reason for encouraging a wider distribution of people was to avoid the mass panic and hysteria that the government feared would be generated by people sheltering in close proximity to one another.

Evacuation actually occurred in three separate stages, with the first beginning on 1 September 1939. Within three days nearly 1.5 million people had been moved. Evacuation did not just take place within Britain; many children were taken overseas to Canada, among other places, before the sinking of two merchant ships carrying large numbers of evacuees put an end to this overseas movement. The first evacuation was characterised by a drift back to the cities, mainly because during the Phoney War parents couldn't see the point of keeping their children away; by January 1940 61 per cent had returned home.

The second wave of evacuation, the so-called 'Trickle Evacuation', was in the summer and autumn of 1940, following the fall of France and the Blitz. It appears to have gone a lot more smoothly, the first evacuation providing a good practice run. Another reason for its success was that the Blitz on many British cities brought the war closer to home, offering a tangible reason for evacuation.

The third phase of evacuation began in June 1944 and was caused by the V1 and V2 attacks on Britain. The first V1 landed in Essex on 13 June 1944, and ½ million people were evacuated from London between the middle of June and the end of July 1944. V2s were first launched in September 1944, and continued their reign of terror until March 1945.

The return of children from evacuation was planned well in advance, with preparations beginning in 1943. Although many had already returned before then, the official homecoming began on 2 May 1945, and was declared complete on 12 July. It was estimated that about 8 million people, including children, mothers, disabled people and overseas refugees were evacuated from cities in Britain, through both government-organised and private schemes.

Education during the Second World War was heavily influenced by the problems of evacuation, but schools also suffered air raid damage and were affected by the conscription of 20,000 male teachers, by the movement of other teaching staff into other war employment, and by the use of many school buildings as rest centres and Civil Defence bases. Schools adapted in many ways to the problems encountered during the war. Some simply carried on, using spaces such as basements to provide safer areas for lessons, and most schools survived the bombings, with only 1,000 of the 23,000 state schools in England and Wales being destroyed. Mercifully, fewer than 7,800 children were killed by air raids throughout the whole of Britain. One of the worst incidents involved a school in Ardgowan Road in Catford, London, in January 1943, when 38 children and 6 teachers were killed.

Many schools were evacuated together, offering their pupils some stability amid the confusion. Camp schools were set up in 1939 in order to avoid the accommodation problems in reception areas. This need to share facilities with other schools, and the war itself, led to a great change in the focus of the school curriculum. Many lessons became a lot more practical and relevant to real life, and also promoted government campaigns as a way to include children in the war effort.

Far from being passive, children contributed in many ways to the success of the war effort. They were encouraged by teachers, parents and MoI campaigns to help in any way they could. Many children became the household fuel-watcher, and they were encouraged to get involved in the National Savings campaign. Most schools had allotments in their grounds, and in this way children were able to

Children from evacuated schools often had to share buildings with others from their school or from different schools. Here children from Woodmansterne Road School in Streatham, London, are sharing the village hall at Farmers in Carmarthenshire. School buildings were often shared by two schools, with one using the facilities in the morning, and the other taking over in the afternoon. *(IWM D 1052)*

contribute to the Dig For Victory campaign. In addition, many children's groups were instrumental in the reuse of bombed areas. One example of this occurred in the East End, where boys trained by the Webbe Boys Club created allotments on bombsites, using seeds donated by the United States. Children also worked in agriculture by helping with the harvest and by picking fruit required by the WVS for jam making either individually or as part of a club or society, such as the Scouts or Guides.

The experiences of children during the Second World War had a huge impact on their lives and it is clear that they involved much more than being herded passively on to trains to the country. Despite some bad times, the evacuees learnt a huge amount about Britain and 'how the other half lived', which hopefully led them to become more rounded adults. The change to more relevant lessons and the focus on the outdoors benefited both the education and the health of the children concerned. In their own way children did their bit for the war effort, through 'Dig for Victory' and National Savings, and so were able to feel that they also had a role on the Home Front.

Opposite above: Children of Chipstead Council School enjoy a physical training lesson led by their teacher Miss Watson in the grounds of South Lodge, c. 1942. The lodge, which adjoined the school, was owned by Mrs Rudolf, who, according to the original caption, 'has taken great interest in the school for 25 years'. PT was a very important part of the curriculum, as was the need for pupils to spend time outdoors. *(IWM D 11031)*

Opposite below: Evacuation provided children with the opportunity to experience aspects of life that were totally different from their usual routine. Here boys from Creek Road LCC School in Greenwich are 'helping' the local blacksmith during their evacuation to Llandissilio in Pembrokeshire, in 1940. *(IWM D 997)*

In addition to the standard evacuation of children, some schools were evacuated to the camp schools set up by the National Camps Corporation under the Camps Act of 1939. Each camp was designed to take about 350 children and provided an outdoor education as well as the standard curriculum. Originally planned to be used by school groups in relays or by holidaymakers in peacetime (and as temporary accommodation for air raid victims), the camps could be said to have solved the problem of the sharing of school premises in reception areas, and provided billets too. The camps were based mainly in the Home Counties, such as those at Marchant's Hill (Hindhead), pictured here, and Sayer's Croft (Ewhurst). Although designed to be temporary, they were later used as Outward Bound centres for London primary schools. *(IWM D 21625)*

Boys of Baldock County Council School in a science lesson, 1944. Baldock School was a senior mixed school, which, according to the original Ministry of Information caption, aimed to provide an education that was 'based on the realities of life and largely non-academic in character'. Of course, traditional subjects were still taught, as this photograph shows, but children were encouraged under the County Badge Scheme to develop their own interests and self-discipline. *(IWM D 20555)*

Above: Children in the village of Knighton-on-Teme in Worcestershire grow vegetables on the school allotments as part of their lessons, 1943. These vegetables would later be harvested and cooked for all in the school to eat. This particular school also provided food for many other schools in the area, and vegetables grown by members of the Village Produce Association also contributed to the school meals provided to local children. *(IWM D 17504)*

Opposite, left to right: Edward Huckstep, Geoffrey Castle, Margaret Romney and Iris Skinner discuss with headteacher Sidney Steele the amount of money they have saved as part of the National Savings Scheme at Blean Village School near Canterbury. Margaret proudly reports the £8 she had collected from her neighbours to Mr Steele. In total the school collected £1,541 in 1940–1. *(IWM D 5023)*

Boys trained by the Webbe Boys Club and supported by the Bethnal Green Bombed Sites Association create an allotment on a bomb site in the East End of London. The seeds they planted were donated by the United States as part of the Lend-Lease scheme. Children were encouraged to 'Dig for Victory' both at home and on the school allotments, and also took part in schemes such as this to regenerate areas that had been badly affected by air raids. *(IWM D 8956)*

Above: Although it was not immediately obvious, children did benefit from the war. Great emphasis was placed on the health of children, an issue that was brought to the fore by rationing, while evacuation illustrated the different lifestyles of youngsters in towns and rural areas. Special rations of orange or blackcurrant juice were given to provide Vitamin C as oranges became scarce. In addition, as we see here, extract of malt and cod liver oil were given to every child. *(IWM D 23618)*

Opposite: Children such as fifteen-year-old George Edward Foster worked in the mining industry before the war, and continued to do so to aid the war effort. George lived in Whinney Hill near Rotherham and worked as a cabin lad. *(IWM D 10159)*

Children contributed to the war effort in many ways. These boy scouts are picking fruit for jam in 1944. As sugar was rationed, jam was extremely important as a source of sweet food; extra rations of sugar were available for those making jam. Many Women's Institute groups made and sold vast quantities. *(IWM D 16206)*

Life for young children was greatly affected by the war, as many were evacuated with their mothers and siblings to other areas of the country. In addition, the schooling of young children developed hugely in the 1930s and 1940s, focusing a great deal on practical skills and outdoor activities. These young children, evacuated to Reading, enjoy a walk in the open air, accompanied, of course, by their gas masks. *(IWM D 824)*

Barbara Hoare feeds the chickens on Mount Batten farm in 1942. Her father Ralph owned the 350 acres of arable land, cattle and poultry that made up the farm. While the rest of the population had to put up with dried egg, chicken farmers enjoyed the privilege of fresh eggs. Poultry farmers and domestic hen-keepers surrendered their dried egg ration and received extra chicken feed instead! *(IWM D 9937)*

CHAPTER 9

OUR FURRY FRIENDS

ANIMALS ON THE

HOME FRONT

Britain has always been a nation of animal lovers, and animals of all kinds have been used by the armed forces during wars. Pigeons, horses and dogs famously served on the battlefields of the First World War, and every ship had its own mascot, ranging from cats, dogs and parrots to goats and even reindeer! Yet they also played a role on the Home Front in the Second World War, and not just as pets.

With petrol rationing and posters asking 'Is your journey really necessary?', the nature of transport changed somewhat, with more reliance on horse-drawn vehicles, even on the streets of London: the Greater London Census of 1937 indicated that there were 40,000 horses in the area. Although passenger transport continued to be fuelled by petrol engines, much of the freight transported on the Home Front was carried by traditional carters and their horses. The idea of salvage was, as we have seen, hugely important at this time, and the rag-and-bone man and his horse-drawn van was a frequent sight on Britain's streets.

Horses had always been used in agriculture, and despite the increased use of tractors during the war, ploughing continued in most cases to be done by horse. Indeed, working horses still out-numbered tractors in 1946.

Police horses also worked hard during the war, with three named Upstart, Olga and Regal, all receiving the Dickin Medal. This medal

Traditional carters and their horses were a common sight on the streets of towns and cities across Britain during the Second World War. Here a London carter transports crates of eggs that have come to Britain under the Lend-Lease scheme. *(IWM D 4328)*

was named after Mrs E. Dickin OBE, founder of the People's Dispensary for Sick Animals (PDSA), and was instituted during the Second World War. It is known as the animals' Victoria Cross and is the highest award that an animal on active service can receive. Also initiated in 1945 was the Silver Medal for animals not on war service that had performed acts of bravery.

Dogs also did their bit for the war effort, with many being employed to sniff out casualties in bomb-damaged buildings. One such dog, Rip, was attached to an ARP post in Southill Street, Poplar, and did his bit as an honorary warden. In addition to helping to locate casualties, Rip also raised a smile from citizens in air raid shelters and supervised his master's work on the ARP post vegetable patch. Rip was one of eight Home Front dogs that won the Dickin Medal for bravery, most of which were awarded for the dogs' work in rescuing people from burning buildings or rubble.

Animals were also important as food, with many people forming pig and rabbit clubs to supplement their rations. Pig clubs were a useful way to use up food scraps, which were fed to pigs that would

Dogs have always been important in warfare, and this Airedale is no exception. In training with the Canadian Army in 1940, this war dog is learning to be a messenger, carrying messages in a pouch attached to his collar. In the same sequence of photographs this dog also learns to carry messenger pigeons in a basket on his back. *(IWM D 440)*

Picked up as a stray by an ARP warden, Rip became one of eight dogs on the Home Front to win the Dickin Medal for bravery. Rip, seen here in December 1941, was a frequent sight around his patch in Poplar, and helped to rescue many people from bombed buildings.
(IWM D 5945)

Pigs make the most of the food scraps fed to them by owner Fred Woolhouse. Mr Woolhouse was a miner and in his spare time cultivated land which he rented from a farmer. Many people already engaged in war work did more to aid the war effort by keeping chickens or pigs, by belonging to pig or rabbit clubs, or by growing vegetables in their back yards and window boxes. (IWM D 8257)

eventually be killed for meat. Over 6,900 pig clubs were in existence by the end of the war, providing their hundreds of thousands of members with extra meat. Pig bins were installed across Britain, and provided a place for kitchen scraps to be collected for use as pig food. Keeping rabbits was also highly profitable, as a single rabbit could produce 2½lb of meat. Our feathered friends were just as important and chickens were extremely popular, providing highly sought-after fresh eggs. It has been estimated that domestic hens provided about a quarter of the country's egg supply in 1943–4, and by 1945 some 12 million chickens were owned by members of the Domestic Poultry Keepers Council.

As more people began to keep animals for food one might think that Britain's fondness for pets had waned, but this was not the case. In the 1937 Greater London Census, only two years before the war,

there were over 400,000 dogs and 1.5 million cats in the greater London area. At the outbreak of war, many people decided to have their pets put down, rather than see them suffer the effects of gas attacks and bombs. Indeed, more than 400,000 dogs and cats were needlessly destroyed in the first few months of war.

The RSPCA advised on gas protection for animals, and had been developing plans for Air Raid Precautions for them as early as 1936. Many volunteer-run rescue centres were in operation during the war, to provide homes for pets whose owners had been made homeless or killed by bombs. Over 700 of these centres existed by 1945.

Clearly then, animals also played their part. As pets they provided a much-needed morale boost to citizens, but they also aided the war effort by transporting goods, seeking out casualties and providing extra food to a heavily rationed population.

In addition to providing entertainment and war news, the wireless was a useful medium for discussing social and political issues. Here in the studio, compère Stanley Maxted, Mrs Vyvyan Adams and a BBC engineer are discussing the broadcast of *Answering You*, c. 1941. (IWM D 4566)

CHAPTER 10

. . . AND RELAX!

HOME LIFE AND
ENTERTAINMENT

Wartime life was not just about the war effort and the constant fear of invasion and air raids: there was also time for fun during the Second World War. The lighter side of life on the Home Front, looking at how people relaxed after a hard day in the factory, the fields or the allotment, has not been forgotten.

Although they had been hugely popular before the war, cinemas took on new status as morale-boosters, disseminators of information and a form of relaxation between 1939 and 1945. All cinemas were closed at the beginning of the war, as it was feared that large groups of people in a public place would provide a target for air raids, but from mid-September 1939 onwards they were allowed to reopen, as long as they were closed by 10 p.m. By December this had been extended to 11 p.m., by which time cinemas were operating almost as normal. Despite the increase in admission prices during the war, each week in Britain between 25 and 30 million tickets were sold, and many people visited the cinema at least once a week, some more frequently.

The cinema offered good value for money. Along with the main feature there was also a B film, a newsreel and a Ministry of Information film related to its current campaign. Many people also visited the cinema in the hope of catching a glimpse of a relative who might be featured in a newsreel about the campaign in North Africa or France. In addition, once the bombs began to fall, cinemas also provided a remarkably good shelter, although sixty London cinemas were destroyed during the war. During air raids many cinema companies re-ran the entire programme or had the organist keep playing in order to

The cinema provided valuable escapism for war workers, enabling them to forget the war once the main feature appeared on screen. Cinemas had been popular before the war, but their status grew beyond all recognition during the war years and queues such as this were a common sight. *(IWM D 25326)*

As now, a visit to the local pub provided people with a place to unwind after a hard day at the factory, and somewhere to discuss the issues of the moment. Glasses of mild (at 5*d* a pint) were the order of the day, and were accompanied by cards, darts, dominoes and singing! *(IWM D 18498)*

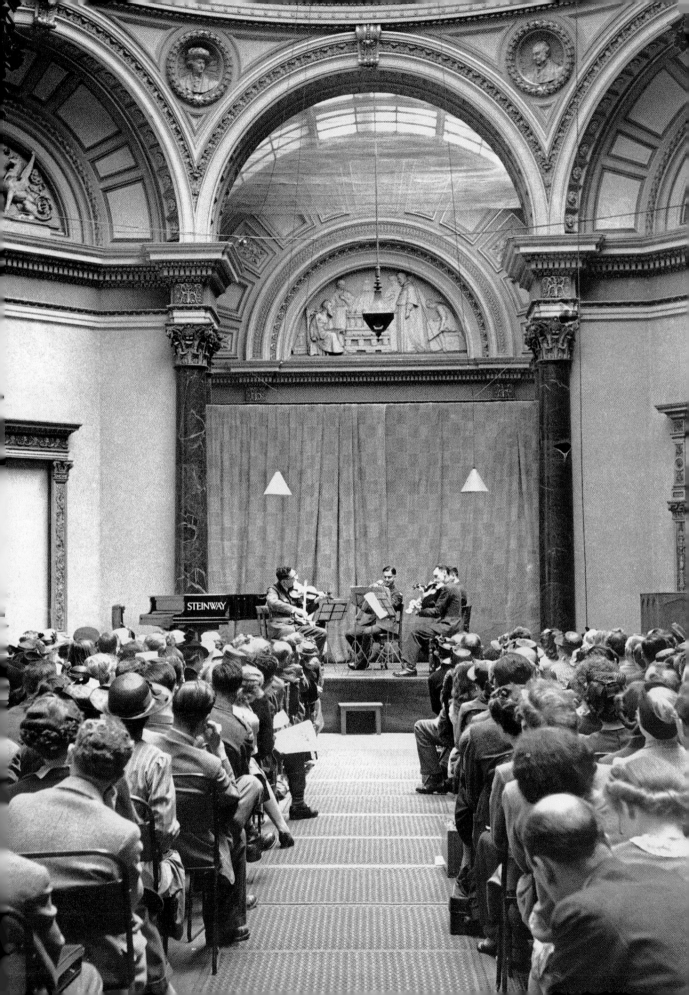

Opposite: Music was a very popular form of entertainment during the Second World War, and concerts such as this one held at the National Gallery in London were frequently put on by the Council for the Encouragement of Music and the Arts (CEMA). Featured here is the Blech String Quartet, with Watson Forbes on viola, playing Mozart's *Quintet for Strings in D Major.* (IWM D 15040)

Above: To keep people up to date with progress on the war's various fronts, mobile cinemas travelled across the length and breadth of the country. Good use was made of time throughout the war, with cinemas being set up in works canteens, such as this one, to ensure that vital time was not wasted by workers watching the war news. (IWM D 18863)

boost the morale of the cinema-goers who were unable to leave the building. People even began to turn up with blankets and food to make a night of it.

The cinema was seen to play such an important part in the upkeep of civilian morale that mobile cinemas were set up and travelled to such places as village halls, so that people in rural areas didn't miss out. As well as providing a much-needed escape from the war effort, the cinema provided a huge opportunity for the MoI to get its point across.

Another popular pre-war pastime that increased in popularity was a visit to the local public house. Pub visiting increased considerably and was spread throughout the week, rather than being concentrated on Friday and Saturday nights, predominantly because of the shift nature of war work. Alcohol consumption in general did not increase but, despite its adulteration with extra water, potatoes and oats, the consumption of beer increased by 25 per cent.

One of the most important forms of escapism and relaxation during the war, for members of the services and civilians alike, was music. Various organisations were created to bring music and the arts to the masses in wartime. CEMA (the Council for the

Encouragement of Music and the Arts) was founded in January 1940. Backed by a government grant, it provided classical concerts and ballets in locations such as the National Gallery, and supported the Old Vic Theatre on its various tours around the country. ENSA (the Entertainments National Service Association) provided concerts and music hall-type shows predominantly to the forces, although concerts were also offered to factory workers. They tended to be a lot more popular and naughty than CEMA, which provided a mostly classical programme.

Another form of music-based entertainment was, of course, dancing. Tea dances were extremely popular and offered people the opportunity to meet new friends and lovers. Many training camps organised dances, which were open to members of the various services, such as those organised by certain groups of the Women's Land Army and attended by US troops.

Probably the most widespread form of entertainment was the radio or wireless. Programmes such as *ITMA* (*It's That Man Again*) and *The Brains Trust* took on a life of their own. *The Brains Trust* proved very popular indeed: starting out in January 1941 it moved up to a peak-time slot, and by 1943 the programme was receiving a regular audience of between 10 and 12 million.

Books also provided great respite from the war effort, despite paper shortages. Book exchanges were set up and page margins were

The Craske family relax after their Sunday lunch by listening to the wireless. Radio was hugely important during the war, keeping the population up to date with news of events both at home and abroad, and also providing much-needed entertainment. Popular programmes such as *It's That Man Again* generated catchphrases that were quoted up and down the country. *(IWM D 12274)*

altered in order to use less paper. More books were bought during the war than ever before, mainly due to the fact that over 400 libraries were damaged by air raids. Inexpensive paperbacks, such as those issued by Penguin from 1935 onwards, enabled people to buy books cheaply and easily. The importance of books is also highlighted by the activities of the Book Repair Depots, which patched up and rebound books for use by the armed forces in Britain and overseas. Libraries were still important, and many factories had them as part of their workers' facilities.

Holidays were also extremely important for service personnel, factory workers and civilians, providing a bit of respite from the rigours of war. Of course, it was necessary to keep public transport as uncluttered by civilian travellers as possible, in order to transport military personnel and supplies more easily. A scheme was therefore developed to encourage people to take 'Holidays at Home'. Many cities competed to encourage visits from the public, with floral displays and concerts forming a large part of their programmes. Parks were extremely popular, particularly Hyde Park in London, which offered open air concerts and boating, as well as the simple pleasures of feeding

Mrs Vyvyan Adams and presenter Vaughan Thomas questioning Mrs Dorothy Hansell and Mr H. Foster during an outside broadcast of *Answering You*, c. 1941. (IWM D 4585)

Reading was a very popular pastime in wartime Britain, and although cheap paper-backs meant that books were purchased in huge numbers, libraries were an essential part of life. Many of the newly built factory complexes that included welfare facilities for war workers also contained a library. *(IWM D 20423)*

Ladies at work at a Services Book Depot in London, 1944. According to the original MoI caption, there were two major depots and several sub-depots, employing a total of 180 people to repair and rebind books for members of the services and up to July 1944 over 130,000 books had been repaired. *(IWM D 21910)*

It was widely recognised that war workers needed periods of rest and relaxation to ensure that both their physical health and their morale were in optimum condition to contribute fully to the war effort. To this end various war workers' hostels, such as this one in Walton-on-the-Hill, Surrey (which opened in March 1944), were set up across Britain, enabling groups of workers to have a complete break from their work, returning, it was hoped, fully refreshed. *(IWM D 20658)*

Children enjoy feeding the ducks in St James's Park as part of the Holidays at Home scheme. London's many parks were a popular destination for both civilians and troops, enabling them to make the most of their free time without putting any extra strain on Britain's already overworked transport systems. *(IWM D 15963)*

Holidays at Home were not just confined to London. All across
Britain people were encouraged to holiday in their local areas
and to enjoy their own gardens. Local beauty spots such as
Jesmond Dene, just outside Newcastle, seen here in about
1943, provided a huge tonic to war workers and local children.
(IWM D 15654)

Sports and physical exercise became increasingly important during the war, as the government aimed to promote widespread health and well-being throughout the population: after all, a healthy workforce is a productive workforce. To this end PT displays were put on in works canteens across the country, demonstrating how quick and easy exercise could be – and fun too. *(IWM D 12991)*

the birds and relaxing on a bench in the sun. Hostels were also provided in stately homes in various areas to provide factory and Civil Defence workers with a relaxing holiday venue.

Although difficult and tiresome at first, certain inconveniences, such as drawing the blackout curtains before switching on lights, queuing for food, living on a meagre ration and recycling everything to within an inch of its life, eventually became routine to people living on the Home Front, and were regarded as an extension to ordinary, everyday life.

Clearly then, home life was altered during the war, as a result of air raids and shortages, yet there was still time, and a deep need, for relaxation. The pub, cinema, theatre and radio seem to have provided the right combination of current affairs and escapism required by the British population during the Second World War, and perhaps this explains why each was so important at this time.

Above: Football has long been the nation's favourite game, and it was no different during the war years. Competitions between various factories were popular, as this photograph demonstrates. Women war workers of A.V. Roe took on their rivals from Fairey Aviation Works (Stockport) at Manchester Athletic Club's Fallowfield Ground in 1944. Fairey won 6–0! *(IWM D 23516)*

Right: Every aspect of life was affected by the war, with many things becoming habitual. One example of this was the blackout. It was essential that the blackout curtain was drawn before any lights were switched on, and any infringement of the blackout would lead to harsh words from the local ARP warden and could also result in a fine. *(IWM D 10588)*

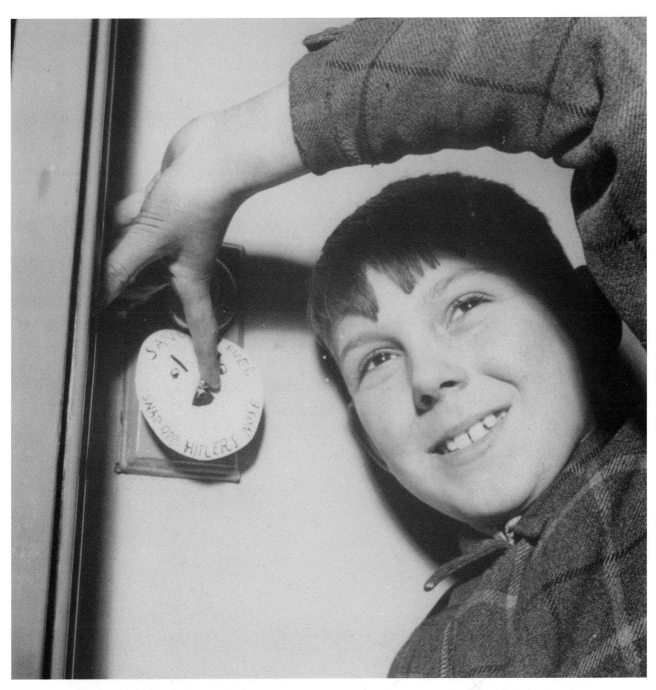

Opposite: Salvage, the need to reuse and recycle everything and a 'Make Do and Mend' mentality were all of huge importance on the Home Front. It became second nature for household rubbish to be separated into piles of kitchen waste, cardboard, paper, glass, tins and rubber, all of which were collected and recycled. Salvage enabled scarce resources to be stretched to their limits and also made people feel that they were contributing to the war effort. *(IWM D 2369)*

Above: Fuel economy was extremely important and was rigorously encouraged by fuel wardens. Children were also encouraged to participate, as part of their contribution to the war effort, as this photograph of a boy 'snapping off Hitler's nose' demonstrates. The electricity saved by switching off lights when not in use saved precious coal. *(IWM D 11087)*

It wasn't just the civilian population that was asked to take part in salvage drives, as illustrated by this huge pile of worn army boots being sorted at a depot. According to the original caption, repairable boots would be mended and resold to civilians, while 'the remainder are sent away with other salvage to be made into fertiliser etc'. *(IWM D 7466)*

Pig bins were an excellent way to avoid wastage of kitchen scraps, such as vegetable peelings. This waste was deposited in special bins set up across the country and then used as pig food. Here Winifred Jordan and Kathleen Kent (head of the Pig Food Collection Unit) of the East Barnet WVS empty a bin into their pig food trailer before driving the 5 miles to the nearest pig farmer. *(IWM D 14248)*

Leading Aircraft Woman Vera Blackbee from Sheerness-on-Sea collects an information leaflet about postwar opportunities after demobilisation at an RAF station in Birmingham. According to the original caption, this station was the only WAAF demob centre in Britain and demobilisation took only 20 minutes. Although women did take advantage of the changed attitude to women in the workplace, many reverted to the traditional role of housewife and mother; indeed by 1951 the proportion of women in employment had reverted to pre-war levels. *(IWM D 25680)*

THE LEGACY
OF WAR

Through the photographs featured in this book an attempt
has been made to illustrate the huge impact that the Second
World War had on life in Britain. The fear of invasion, the
awful realities of air raids, the blackout, rationing and the evacuation
of children were all hugely important and all left their mark on the
psyche of Home Front citizens.

The role of the MoI in recording these events, and more
importantly in making sure that the public was fully behind the war
effort, is exemplified through the photographs. The MoI held sway
over every single aspect of life between 1939 and 1945, influencing
everything from basic necessities such as the clothing worn by people
of all ages, to the types of food eaten (and even the crockery from
which that food was consumed), to more fundamental issues such as
the mechanisation of agriculture, the growth of British industry and
the role of women in society. Indeed, although today we take for
granted our education system, the National Health Service and even
the shape of our cities (thanks to bomb damage and postwar town
planning), they all have their roots in the Second World War, and the
long-term effects of that conflict are still very much in evidence
today.

All these issues are highlighted and celebrated in the photographs
in the 'D Series', and in its way the Ministry of Information still has
some influence over us today, supplying us with its own particular
vision of life in Britain during the Second World War.

Right and below: Throughout the war the government, through the MoI, had attempted to control (or at least to strongly influence) the health and well-being of British citizens, predominantly to aid the success of the war effort. This focus on the importance of health continued into the postwar period, with the passing of the National Health Service Act in 1946 leading to the creation of the National Health Service on 5 July 1948. These photographs show an MoI exhibition held on behalf of the Ministry of Health at Charing Cross station in 1945. The desire to create a free-for-all health service had long been mooted, but the nationalisation of many of Britain's services during the war no doubt crystallised these efforts. *(IWM D 19233 / D 19235)*

After six years of military service it was time for personnel of the people's war to return to civvy street. Here RSM C. Stilwell is being measured for his demob suit at the Clothing Depot at Olympia, London, on 18 June 1945, after being officially demobbed at the No. 4 Military Dispersal Centre, Regent's Park. *(IWM D 26324)*

The destruction of many homes by German bombs necessitated the construction of new ones. The sheer numbers required meant that it was not possible to begin building a series of permanent residences, so instead a programme was started to create large numbers of temporary homes. Here is the Persian Press Delegation inspecting the construction of temporary houses in London's East End in 1945. *(IWM D 26229)*

A scale-model of the proposed developments to Portsmouth. Towns such as Portsmouth and Coventry, which had been severely damaged during air raids, were extensively rebuilt after the war, with many areas developing on the planning ideas of the early 1930s, aiming to create more open space and buildings designed for specific purposes. (IWM D 21921)

THE GREATER LONDON PLAN PROPOSES EIGHT NEW SATELLITE TOWNS

Ten possible sites for these towns—in the Outer Country Ring or just beyond it—are indicated. From these, eight would be selected.

THE SITES ARE:

Stevenage	Margaretting
Redbourn	Meopham
Stapleford	Crowhurst
Harlow	Holmwood
Ongar	White Waltham

In most of these new towns a population of about 60,000 is proposed.

To show how one of the new satellite towns might be laid out, a detailed plan and a model have been made of the proposed town of Ongar.

THE PROPOSED SATELLITE TOWN OF ONGAR

The village of Chipping Ongar is in the Outer Country Ring, 21½ miles as the crow flies from Charing Cross.

The Greater London Plan proposes

The old village should form the centre of the new town.

Six neighbourhoods, each largely self-contained, should be grouped on the hills surrounding the old village.

The railway to London should be electrified and industry sited in a valley through which the railway would be extended.

The existing parklands should be preserved and the flood lands of the Roding drained to form playing fields.

Longer-term town planning began during the war, and many saw the Blitz as an opportunity to create new communities. The Town and Country Planning Act of 1944 aimed to rebuild areas that had been devastated by bombs. This exhibition on the Greater London Plan (part of two papers known as the Abercrombie Plan after Professor Patrick Abercrombie) was held in London in 1945 and emphasised the desire to create more open space. After the war the New Towns Act (1 August 1946) led to the creation of several 'New Towns', the first of these being Stevenage on 11 November 1946.
(IWM D 25773)

BIBLIOGRAPHY

Balfour, Michael, *Propaganda in War 1939–1945, Organisations, Policies and Publics in Britain and Germany*, Routledge & Kegan Paul, 1979

Billingham, Elizabeth, *Civil Defence in War*, John Murray & the Pilot Press, 1941

Bourne, Dorothea St Hill, *They Also Serve*, Winchester Publications, 1947

Briggs, Susan, *Keep Smiling Through: Britain, 1939–1945*, Book Club Associates, 1975

Calder, Angus, *The People's War*, Pimlico, 1969

——, *The Myth of the Blitz*, Jonathan Cape, 1991

Cooper, Jilly, *Animals in War*, Corgi, 2000

Craig, Charles, *The British Documentary Photograph as a Medium of Information and Propaganda during the Second World War 1939–1945*, thesis sponsored by Middlesex Polytechnic in collaboration with the Imperial War Museum, 1982

Crang, Jeremy A., *The British Army and the People's War 1939–1945*, Manchester University Press, 2000

Davies, Jennifer, *The Wartime Kitchen and Garden: The Home Front 1939–45*, BBC Books, 1993

Dickinson, Margaret and Street, Sarah, *Cinema and State: The Film Industry and the British Government 1927–84*, British Film Institute, 1985

Dover, Harriet, *Home Front Furniture: British Utility Design 1941–1951*, Scolar Press, 1991

Drummond, John D., *Blue for a Girl: the Story of the WRNS*, W.H. Allen, 1960

Gardiner, Juliet, *'Over Here': the GIs in Wartime Britain*, Collins & Brown, 1992

Gosden, P.H.J.H., *Education in the Second World War: a Study in Policy and Administration*, Methuen, 1976

Gregg, John, *The Shelter of the Tubes: Tube Sheltering in Wartime London*, Capital Transport, 2001

Haldane, J.B.S., *ARP*, Victor Gollancz, 1938

HMSO, *Persuading the People*, HMSO, 1995

Holman, Bob, *The Evacuation: a Very British Revolution*, Lion Publishing, 1995

Hylton, Stuart, *Their Darkest Hour: the Hidden History of the Home Front 1939–1945*, Sutton Publishing, 2001

Le Chêne, Evelyn, *Silent Heroes: the Bravery and Devotion of Animals in War*, Souvenir Press, 1994

Lewis, Peter, *A People's War*, Thames Methuen, 1986

Longmate, Norman, *How We Lived Then: A History of Everyday Life During the Second World War*, Hutchinson, 1971

Lynn, Vera (with Robin Cross and Jenny de Gex), *We'll Meet Again: a Personal and Social Memory of World War Two*, Sidgwick & Jackson, 1989

Mackay, Robert, *The Test of War: Inside Britain 1939–45*, UCL, 1999

Marwick, Arthur, *The Home Front: the British and the Second World War*, Thames & Hudson, 1976

Mass Observation, *War Begins at Home*, Chatto & Windus, 1940

——, *The Pub and the People: a Worktown Study*, Victor Gollancz, 1943

McDowell, Colin, *Forties Fashion and the New Look*, Bloomsbury, 1997

McLaine, Ian, *Ministry of Morale: Home Front Morale and the Ministry of Information in World War II*, George Allen & Unwin, 1979

Minister of National Defence, *The Canadians in Britain*, 1946

Ministry of Home Security, *Front Line 1940–41 – the Official Story of the Civil Defence of Britain*, HMSO, 1942

Ministry of Labour and National Service, *Women in Industry*, 1945

Moss, Arthur W. & Kirby, Elizabeth, *Animals Were There: A Record of the Work of the RSPCA from 1939–1945*, Hutchinson, 1946

National Council of Social Service, *British Restaurants: An Inquiry*, Geoffrey Cumberlege, Oxford University Press, 1946

O'Brien, Terence, *Civil Defence*, HMSO and Longmans, Green, 1955

Sackville West, Vita, *The Women's Land Army*, Imperial War Museum, 1944 and 1993

Sladen, Christopher, *The Conscription of Fashion: Utility Cloth, Clothing and Footwear 1941–1952*, Scolar Press, 1995

Smith, Graham, *When Jim Crow met John Bull: Black American Soldiers in World War II Britain*, IB Tauris, 1987

Spender, Stephen, *Citizens in War – and After*, George G. Harrap, 1945

Turner, E.S., *The Phoney War on the Home Front*, Michael Joseph, 1961

Tyrer, Nicola, *They Fought in the Fields. The Women's Land Army: The Story of a Forgotten Victory*, Sinclair-Stevenson, 1996

Wallington, Neil, *Firemen at War: The Work of London's Fire-fighters in the Second World War*, David & Charles, 1981

Ziegler, Philip, *London At War 1939–1945*, Sinclair-Stevenson, 1995

INDEX